Praise for *Brilliant Teaching Assistant*

'A good introduction to twenty-first-century schools and the varied role of a TA.'

Liz Kidd, teaching assistant

'This is an invaluable reference book for all teaching assistants, covering broad aspects of the role. The practical case studies and further references and resources are particularly helpful.'

Liz Wiltshire, teaching assistant

'*Brilliant Teaching Assistant* – what a brilliant book! Provides the reader with a concise point of reference for all those important questions you need answered – but didn't know who to ask! Appropriate for aspiring teaching assistants, school volunteers and any adult who has the privilege of supporting teaching and learning in our schools.'

Kim O'Rourke, CPD co-ordinator supporting teaching and learning, Wiltshire

'This comprehensive guide covers everything a teaching assistant should know in simplistic, manageable chapters – essential reading for every teaching assistant!'

Tracey Perks, teaching assistant

D0715189

467 438 53 3

brilliant

teaching
assistant

teaching
assistant

What you need to know to be a truly
outstanding teaching assistant

Louise Burnham

Prentice Hall
is an imprint of

Harlow, England • London • New York • Boston • San Francisco • Toronto • Sydney • Singapore • Hong Kong
Tokyo • Seoul • Taipei • New Delhi • Cape Town • Madrid • Mexico City • Amsterdam • Munich • Paris • Milan

PEARSON EDUCATION LIMITED

Edinburgh Gate
Harlow CM20 2JE
Tel: +44 (0)1279 623623
Fax: +44 (0)1279 431059
Website: www.pearsoned.co.uk

First published in Great Britain in 2011

Pearson Education is not responsible for the content of third party internet sites.

ISBN: 978-0-273-73442-0

British Library Cataloguing-in-Publication Data
A catalogue record for this book is available from the British Library

Library of Congress Cataloging-in-Publication Data
Burnham, Louise.
    Brilliant teaching assistant : what you need to know to be a truly outstanding teaching assistant / Louise Burnham.
        p. cm.
    Includes index.
    ISBN 978-0-273-73442-0 (pbk.)
    1. Teachers' assistants--Great Britain.   I. Title.
    LB2844.1.A8B88 2011
    371.14'124--dc22
                                                2010050961

10 9 8 7 6 5 4
15 14 13 12

Typeset in 10/14pt Plantin by 3
Printed and bound in Great Britain by Henry Ling Limited, at the Dorset Press, Dorchester, DT1 1HD

For Richard, with love.

Contents

About the author

Louise Burnham has worked as an Early Years and primary teacher, SENCO (Special Educational Needs Co-ordinator) and teaching assistant manager in several primary schools. She led teaching assistant training for a number of years at a south London college before going back into school, where she now teaches part time as well as continuing to work with teaching assistants and students of Early Years.

Acknowledgements

I would like to thank the many teaching assistants I have met and had the opportunity to work with over the past few years whose inspiring work, ideas and discussions have enabled me to write this book. I would also like to thank the following people for their contributions: Val Hughes and Sandhurst Junior School in Catford for a copy of their TA feedback sheet; Downderry School in Downham for a copy of their accident report form; Frances Rickford, Liz Wiltshire, Tracey Perks and Kim O'Rourke for reading through the manuscript; and Katy Robinson at Pearson Education for her feedback and patience during the writing of this book.

Foreword

Teaching assistants play a crucial role in today's schools. Or, to be more accurate, they play many crucial roles. Their number literally doubled between 2000 and 2010, to 190,000 full-time equivalent jobs – and that's only in England. There are lots of reasons for this rapid growth, but one of the main causes was the move to free up more teachers' time for teaching. The Workforce Remodelling Agreement, signed by the government and most education unions in 2003, created the conditions for support staff to take over many non-teaching tasks from teachers – tasks such as preparing classrooms for lessons, making displays and invigilating exams, collecting dinner money and photocopying. Higher Level Teaching Assistant status was introduced so that teaching assistants who could show they had the right skills would be able to take on extra responsibilities, and get a higher rate of pay.

As well as supporting teachers, teaching assistants are also needed in large numbers to support children with special educational needs. David Blunkett, Tony Blair's first Education Secretary, had painful childhood memories of being sent away to blind school himself and was determined that disabled children should go to mainstream schools. Many of these children need extra support to be able to join in with their classmates' activities and fully benefit from everything school has to offer.

Whatever the reason, the fact is that most schools now employ several teaching assistants, and most classes now have more than one adult present at least some of the time. Teaching assistants, under the supervision of the teacher, support the learning of hundreds of thousands of pupils every day, individually, in groups, or in whole classes.

Equally importantly, they take care of children's emotional and social needs. Whether they're working in the playground or in school, teaching assistants tend to have more one-to-one contact than teachers with individual children, and children look to them for support and comfort with problems at home as well as at school.

Although there are no minimum qualifications for being a teaching assistant, more and more schools want qualified teaching assistants, and there has been a confusing array of qualifications available. The new unit-based Qualification and Credit Framework should mean teaching assistants can build up a qualification at their own pace, and don't have to spend time studying things they already know.

Nonetheless, even with a qualification, going into a new school as a teaching assistant can be a daunting experience. One of the trickiest challenges is to work out who's who, and how to build the right relationships with pupils and colleagues alike. *Brilliant Teaching Assistant* offers plenty of down-to-earth guidance on how schools really work, and where you fit in, and the case studies and examples pose some of the knotty, practical problems a teaching assistant is likely to encounter in the real world. Louise Burnham doesn't offer simplistic solutions, but by bringing the reader the benefit of her own experience as a TA trainer and a Special Educational Needs Co-ordinator, she's written a solid and practical introduction for anyone thinking of becoming a teaching assistant, starting a new TA job, or wanting some extra inspiration in their current TA role.

Frances Rickford
Editor
Learning Support *magazine*
www.learningsupport.co.uk

Introduction

Why become a teaching assistant?

'We get all the best bits!'

'We get all the joys of teaching but without the hassle'

'We get to spend time with the children and have time to talk to them'

'It's great, it's fun and I can just go into work and go home again without having to do too much preparation'

'It's great to be in the school environment and we don't have the same pressure as teachers'

All of the above quotes were given by teaching assistants working in schools. If you have bought this book, you are interested in finding out whether you are or could become a Brilliant Teaching Assistant. This may be for a number of reasons:

- because you are new to the role;
- because you would like to find out more about what similarities and differences there are between jobs and schools;
- because you may be thinking about taking the plunge and going back into work or training after a career break.

Alternatively, you may be quite experienced and want to find out more about different aspects of what teaching assistants do and broaden your horizons even further. Whatever your reasons, you will want to look at the range of opportunities available to you and consider how teaching assistants can really make a difference to pupils in many ways. From supporting teaching and learning to mentoring and providing a listening ear to pupils, teaching assistants are a vital part of the whole school team.

Support staff have always been in schools, but in 2002 the government started to give large amounts of funding to 'professionalising' their role and making specific qualifications available. According to data released in May 2010 by the Department for Education, the total number of teaching assistants in local authority-maintained English schools rose from 79,000 in 2000 to 190,000 in 2009. The impact of this has been huge and has meant that in some schools, the number of teaching assistants is now almost as high as the number of teachers.

Teaching assistants are now qualified to different levels, from HLTAs (Higher Level Teaching Assistants), Level 2 and 3 NVQs (at around GCSE and A level) in Supporting Teaching and Learning in Schools. Teaching assistants have also been able to undertake the Support Work in Schools (SWiS) qualification which has been available to anyone in school who works as a member of support staff. At the time of writing further new qualifications are being developed. Teaching assistants may also have a specialism in areas of special educational needs (SEN), or take intervention groups with specific pupils. This means that they will often have precise responsibilities, be part of a curriculum area, or have to plan, teach and assess pupils independently whilst reporting back to teachers.

As an 'extra pair of hands' in the classroom, teaching assistants are now an essential part of the school team and one which most teachers can seldom do without. Although this change has been gradual, the different roles which have evolved are now hugely varied and assistants are now taken on with widely differing job descriptions – something which would not have happened 10 or 15 years ago. Teaching assistants may work in a number of different roles in one school, or have different jobs in different places. Consider the examples below.

▶ brilliant examples

Sarah

Sarah works in a large secondary school alongside 20 other teaching assistants and individual support assistants (ISAs). She has a Maths degree and works closely with the Maths teacher, preparing resources and supporting both gifted and talented groups in the lower school and those working below age expectations in Years 10 and 11.

Carole

Carole works in a two-form entry primary school and supports the class teacher in Year 1 during the mornings. She arrives at school at 8.45 and speaks briefly to the teacher before working alongside small groups for literacy. She then spends afternoons with different year groups as she supports the ICT technician and various class teachers. This gives her the opportunity to develop her interest in ICT.

Ian

Ian works in a small village primary school. He arrives at school at 7.30 and helps with breakfast club until school starts. He then works in Year 6 supporting literacy and numeracy groups in the morning before covering lunchtime. He then goes home. After school he comes back to work with after school club.

Whatever your role, you will need to be able to turn your hand to most things in school – this may be anything from dealing with an injured or distressed pupil to invigilating exams or organising costumes for the Christmas play. However, as you become more experienced you will probably find there are some areas you are more comfortable with, and be able to express your interest. This is one of the great advantages of your job – you should be able to develop areas in which you have a particular strength or enthusiasm! This book will guide you through these different aspects of your role and also those of others in your school team so that you can see how you fit in to the school as a whole. It also provides several Brilliant case studies, the solutions to which can be found in Appendix 1.

CHAPTER 1

Working effectively as part of the whole school team

When you first start in your new job you may be bewildered by the different titles which exist to describe the role of a teaching assistant. You may be known as an Individual Support Assistant (ISA), Learning Support Assistant (LSA) or Classroom Assistant. If you have a higher level qualification you may be employed as a Higher Level Teaching Assistant (HLTA). Although these are all slightly different, 'teaching assistant' is the generic term to cover all the different aspects of the role. In some local authorities (LAs), those with different qualifications are given titles according to the level they have reached, but this is regional and will depend on where you are in the country. Whatever your role, it is important that you understand where and how you fit into the school team, so that you can maximise your effectiveness and that of those around you (see table overleaf).

What is a 'whole school team?'

There have been many models and breakdowns of how school teams fit together, and each school will be different, depending on whether it is a primary, secondary or special school, and how teams are managed within this. However, broadly speaking, all schools will have a governing body and a senior management team which supervises

> all schools will have a governing body and a senior management team

Teaching assistant	The generic term for anyone who supports teaching and learning in school.
Classroom assistant	As above, anyone who supports teaching and learning in school.
Individual Support Assistant (ISA)	This means that the assistant is allocated to work with a particular child, for example one who has special educational needs.
Learning Support Assistant/Special Support Assistant	As above, an assistant working with a named child.
Bilingual assistants	May work with pupils who do not speak the target language (i.e. English or Welsh). It may be necessary to use the pupil's first language to support them and to help assess their educational abilities. Bilingual assistants may also work with families and liaise with them in order to promote pupil participation.
Learning mentor	This role has evolved as usually a teaching assistant who works closely with a pupil in order to overcome barriers to learning. They will usually work as a listener, role model and advisor to pupils.
Family worker	This role has been developed as a result of the Every Child Matters framework in order to support children and young people and their families. Family workers will often be teaching assistants who liaise with families and the wider community and provide guidance on parenting, health issues and counselling, signposting families to outside agencies where needed. This role will usually be taken on by a more experienced assistant.
HLTA	A teaching assistant who has achieved higher level teaching assistant status.

a team of teachers and teaching assistants along with other support staff (see Figure 1.1). Within the different teams, line managers will exist for staff and you will need to know who yours is: as a teaching assistant it is unlikely that your line manager will be the headteacher – it is more likely to be the deputy headteacher, Special Educational Needs Co-ordinator (SENCO), or possibly an HLTA.

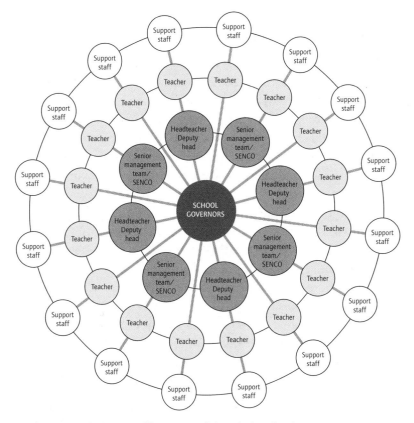

Figure 1.1 Support staff are part of the whole school team

Source: Burnham, L. (2007) *S/NVQ Level 3 The Teaching Assistant's Handbook: Primary Schools*

The governing body

The governing body will be made up of a team of around ten or twelve people who meet regularly and have close contact with the headteacher and senior management team. They will usually have areas of expertise which may be in the financial, legal or business world and will be from the local community. There will also be staff and parent governors – if you have time and you are interested in becoming a governor, this is worth doing as it gives a real insight into how the school is run.

The governing body will also be responsible for carrying out the headteacher's performance management interview (the annual review of the headteacher's professional targets). He or she will report to governors about the running of the school and is answerable to them about all aspects of it from financial management, site management, community cohesion (see page 134) and the curriculum, to employing new staff. With this in mind, the governing body will be split into different committees of around four members and will meet once or twice a term. They will then feed back to the main governing body once a term. Minutes of these meetings should be available to all staff and parents if requested. The headteacher will also produce an annual report to them about what has been achieved during the previous year. Governors may be completely invisible to you but they should really make themselves known to all staff and children and should come regularly into school during the school day to see it in action, rather than just in the evenings for meetings – although this may be difficult in the real world!

The SMT or Senior Management Team

In all schools this team will meet regularly with the headteacher and deputy to discuss priorities in the school and to identify current issues in the school development plan (the school development plan, or SDP, is a document which usually spans four or five years and sets out the overall priorities and plans for the school). You should be aware of who the senior managers are in your school and what their responsibilities are. The team will usually include the headteacher, deputy, SENCO, and year group leaders, but may also include other managers (for example, the Foundation Stage manager, if you are in an infant school). Senior managers will support the headteacher in decisions concerning the school and ensure that information is passed on to all staff.

The SENCO

The SENCO (Special Educational Needs Co-ordinator) is responsible for managing the provision for pupils with special educational needs. They will need to meet and liaise with staff, parents and outside agencies and may be your line manager if you are working as an individual support assistant. (For more on the role of the SENCO see Chapter 5, pages 88–9.)

Year group leaders

Year group leaders are found both in primary and secondary schools, and are literally the lead teacher in that year group. They will usually be a member of the senior management team (SMT) and will feed back information to their year group at their own meetings, usually held weekly. Year group leaders will usually be the most experienced permanent member of staff in that team and so will be able to advise and support others in the team. They will also give guidance towards planning and assessment and make sure that resources are available to all (for example, in a primary school where classes in a year group are working on the same topic).

Subject leaders

These are teachers within both primary and secondary schools who have responsibility for a subject area. They will advise and support other staff in the planning, assessment, resourcing and teaching of the subject area. They will also monitor how it is taught in school and may carry out lesson observa-

> these are teachers who have responsibility for a subject area

tions or ask how things are going. They may also be useful to identify as you may be able to seek advice from them if you work regularly with a particular subject.

As well as giving advice to staff within the school, subject leaders may also be involved in working with other schools at local authority level to develop their subject. They will probably attend termly local meetings to keep up to date with any developments in their subject so that they can feed these back to school staff. Teaching assistants may also work closely with subject leaders if they are specialists in a particular area, as is sometimes the case in secondary schools.

Support staff

This will usually be quite a large group of people and, although you will be part of it, depending on the size of your school you may not meet with a wider group than other teaching assistants. However, support staff are made up of all other non-teaching staff in schools – i.e. office or admin staff, site managers, kitchen staff, ICT technicians, business managers, midday supervisors and others. Support staff will sometimes work part time and you may not know everyone if you are also only in school on certain days. If not, it will help to try to get to know others on occasions where everyone *is* in school, such as INSET days, or perhaps at more social school events when these take place.

As well as the above broad headings, you will probably find that there are smaller sub-groups, for example midday supervisors, or newly qualified teachers (NQTs), who may meet together or spend more time with one another than the wider group.

brilliant example

David is an individual support assistant in a secondary school. He is new to the role and is line managed by the school's SENCO. He has meetings with different teams within the school:

● David meets with the SENCO both to discuss the pupil he works with and to clarify anything which comes up as he settles into school.

- He also meets with other ISAs and teaching assistants once a fortnight at lunchtime to find out about whole school issues.

- Occasionally, the whole school staff will meet together for staff training or INSET days.

Whatever teams or groups you are part of, you should be able to contribute to their effectiveness and work alongside others for the benefit of pupils. You will also need to be able to contribute in your own way to the development of the team through providing support and advice to others. If you are lucky enough to work in a school where all staff members work together positively, you will find this very supportive to you in your role.

brilliant tip

If you are new to a school, take a few moments to work out your own school's staff structure and who in the school is responsible for different areas. The office will probably have some kind of staff list which will identify names for you. Make sure you know who the key members of staff are and those which may be particularly relevant for you. Some schools will even have handy photographs of key staff on the wall in the entrance area which, although useful, is not always popular!

Working with others

Working with others will include how you relate to parents, teachers, and other school staff. You may also work closely with other professionals who visit the school. As you will be working in different teams it is worth thinking about how your role fits in with that of others and how you are able to support them.

Depending on your experience, you will bring a unique level of expertise to the school. You may have had specific training and be able to advise others. If you have information or expertise

which would benefit others in your team, you should support others by passing on anything which may be useful. In some schools you

| you will bring a unique |
| level of expertise |

may be required to feed back information on courses you have attended through meetings, or if you are experienced, you may be working with others who would benefit from some of your ideas – this could also be done more informally.

🡵 brilliant case study

Emma has just spent break talking to Lorraine, who is another teaching assistant working in Key Stage 2. She has found some challenges in her work with a particular pupil in the class that Lorraine supported the previous year. Lorraine is able to talk through some of the strategies which worked and which she may find useful.

● In what ways will this chat be useful?

● How else might Lorraine be able to help Emma in the long term?

You may be less experienced and find that you are in a situation where you need advice and support – do not be afraid of asking for it. There will usually be someone in school who has dealt with a similar situation or who may put a different slant on things.

Working with other support staff within the same classroom

This may be surprising, but you might find yourself working in a class where there are a number of different support staff who have varying roles. An example of this might be in a classroom where there is more than one pupil who has an area of special educational need. Although it is always beneficial for the pupil, it may at times be difficult for adults to know exactly what their role is. It will be necessary in this situation to meet with teachers, the SENCO or the other individuals concerned and talk through how pupils are supported within the class on a regular basis. You should also discuss how much time you should spend with the individual pupil on specific targets and how much time you can spend on group work. This is particularly important in situations where more than one assistant is working with a pupil (for example, if one person is with them in the morning and another in the afternoon).

Working alongside teachers

This really is the key part of your role. You will need to be able to get the best out of the time available with the staff with whom you are working so that you can work together for the benefit of pupils. At the beginning of each year it would be useful to sit down with key staff and plan out whether you will have time to meet, what kind of information would be useful to you and how you might best work together in your particular situation. Some teaching assistants literally have no time to plan with or talk to teachers and

> get the best out of the time available with the staff

walk into class on a regular basis with no idea what is being taught that day – this is clearly not ideal for anyone. In these circumstances it would make sense for teachers to email plans to teaching assistants if time is short – at least then the lesson or support required will not be a surprise on the day. You should also have the opportunity to feed back to teachers on how pupils you have supported have worked during lessons so that they are able to plan effectively for next time – again, if this is not possible in the time available you may consider using feedback forms (see also Chapter 3, page 41).

Working with parents

All staff working in schools will need to be able to relate to parents. Although the main point of contact for parents will be teachers, if you are working as a teaching assistant you may well have regular meetings or points of contact with them at the beginning or end of the school day. This may be particularly relevant if you are, for example, the school's family worker, if you support a pupil who has special educational needs, or are working with a bilingual pupil. You should make sure that you stay on subject when talking to parents and that you are mindful of confidentiality issues (see opposite).

It is also important not to take things into your own hands; if you think that the parent has asked something which is more appropriate for a teacher to deal with, you must say so and refer to them. Don't be drawn into something which you do not feel confident in discussing. If you are a family worker you should have had specific training about how you relate to families and the advice and support you should provide.

Managing conflict

Working with others, in whatever profession you choose, will sometimes be great and at other times difficult, and you are bound to get on with some people more than others. At some point in your career it is likely that you will find yourself having to work with a personality which may be very different from your own. This may be a teacher but it is also possible that you will have to work regularly with another professional, or a parent, particularly if you are supporting a child who has special educational needs. If you anticipate finding them hard to work with it is important to remember that it is probably for a relatively short time and that you may well learn a lot by working with that person. You should remain professional at all times and, where issues arise in the workplace, talk them through with the relevant person, such as your line manager.

You will also need to be sensitive at times to others' needs – all members of staff in schools will have a lot on their mind and you may not be aware what pressures they are under as part of their job. Many will have families and issues to deal with outside school, which at times can also have an impact on their ability to provide the same level of support. You should also try to be self-aware and think about the way in which you relate to others in your team, as it may be that you do not always come across in the way that you think. If someone is not reacting to you in a positive way, could it be because of something you have said to them?

If you find yourself in a conflict situation with another individual this will need to be addressed as soon as possible. Although rare, these issues do occasionally happen and you may need to have a meeting with another adult present in order to discuss a way forward. Be particularly careful if you are alone with another person – if you are not comfortable, and the other person is being aggressive or abusive in some way, move to a different place or tell them that you are not prepared to discuss the situation without a mediator. If the conflict is more of a low level disagreement and is ongoing, you should always seek additional help and refer to your school's grievance policy.

As an adult in a school environment, you must remember that you are a role model and are responsible for showing pupils positive relationships. Pupils will witness how adults interact with one another and work together and take their lead from them. If they see adults being considerate and appreciative of others, it is far more likely that they will behave in the same way.

> you must remember that you are a role model

Remembering confidentiality

When you start your job it is likely that your line manager or headteacher will speak to you about the importance of confidentiality in school. This is particularly relevant to you as a teaching assistant because, in many cases, teaching assistants are also parents, often of pupils in the same school. The most important thing to remember is not to speak about pupils or staff to those who do not work in the school, and if in doubt about whether you should say something – don't!

↗ brilliant case study

Sina works in a small village primary school as a teaching assistant in Year 2. Her child is in another class and her best friend is also a parent at the school. Sina's friend regularly tries to find out what happens in the class on a daily basis and often questions her on the way home about specific children. She is also very keen that her child is put up to the next level in reading and asks Sina to 'sort it out' for her.

- What should Sina do in this situation?
- Why is it important that she does not talk to her friend about what happens in class?

✗ brilliant dos and don'ts

Do

✔ Embrace differences – it would be very boring if we were all the same!

✔ Acknowledge the support and ideas of others.

✔ Always try to talk differences through rationally as they arise.

✔ Try to attend the occasional social event which staff attend.

Don't

✗ Get caught up in an argument, particularly in front of pupils.

✗ Gossip or talk about others negatively in the workplace.

✗ Breach confidentiality.

School policies

All schools are required to have a number of different policies which are designed to support the smooth running of the school. These will be divided into curriculum and non-curriculum areas and should be revised and updated on a regular basis. Your line manager will be able to tell you where you need to go to refer to them – probably in the school office, and sometimes they may even be on the school's website so that parents can look at them easily. Everyone who works in the school should also be aware of where to find them and should have some idea about the content of each. A list of the policies which you should know about and be able to find are given below:

- health and safety policy;
- behaviour policy;
- child protection policy;
- marking policy;
- inclusion/equal opportunities policy.

You should also know your school's SEN policy if you are working with pupils who have special educational needs, the Foundation Stage or Early Years policy if you are working in reception, and so on. If you are working in a specific curriculum area – for example, in the History department – you should ensure that you have read the appropriate curriculum policy. Your line manager will be able to talk to you about anything which may need clarification.

brilliant tip

Be aware of where the school keeps its policies so that you can refer to them if necessary.

brilliant recap

- All schools will be structured in a similar way but within this there may be slight differences.

- There will be a number of different teams within the whole school structure and you may be part of more than one of these – for example, subject area teams, support staff teams, year group teams. Make sure you know where you fit in.

- When working with others remember to be professional at all times.

CHAPTER 2

The school curriculum, timetabling and planning

As a member of staff who supports teaching and learning, you will need to have some awareness of the curriculum you are supporting, its structure and how different types of planning fit together. Although many areas of the curriculum are at the time of writing undergoing a period of change, the principle of knowing and understanding the key areas of learning in whatever subject area you are supporting remains just as important, and you should be entitled to additional training if the curriculum of the age group you are supporting changes radically.

Whilst some teaching assistants may be closely involved in planning with teachers, others may have no input, sight of plans or idea about what they will be doing until they are asked to support teaching and learning activities with individuals or groups. You will need to try to work with teachers to ensure that you know as much as possible in advance about the

> work with teachers to ensure that you know as much as possible

lessons you will be supporting so that all pupils have full access to the curriculum for their age and stage.

The school curriculum 4–16

The national curriculum

In 1988, the Education Reform Act changed the way in which the curriculum was delivered in England and Wales when the then government introduced a national curriculum. This was designed so that all state schools would have guidance as to the content of what was expected to be taught and for ease of planning and assessment.

Since 1988 the curriculum has been through some changes and is regularly updated, and different countries of the UK now have their own distinct curricula. However, at the time of writing, the national curriculum in England at primary and secondary level is divided into specific subjects which relate to both statutory and non-statutory frameworks (see Table 2.1). The national curriculum is statutory in all state schools and, whilst the various subject areas are important, the non-statutory guidance covers aspects of education which support a pupil's overall development and general achievement. These are areas such as Personal, Social and Health Education (PSHE) – which may be made a statutory area in the future – economic wellbeing, sex and relationship education, careers education and so on. Although these areas are non-statutory, they are an essential part of the pupils' school experience as they will enhance learning and development.

From Year 1 onwards the national curriculum is comprised of:

● Key Stage 1: Years 1 and 2 (sometimes still called 'infants');
● Key Stage 2: Years 3 and 4 (sometimes still called 'juniors').

At secondary school, the curriculum is set out in different stages:

● Key Stage 3: Years 7–9;
● Key Stage 4: Years 10 and 11;
● Post-16 (sixth form).

In Key Stage 4, pupils are also entitled to study subjects such as Design and Technology, Modern Foreign Languages, Humanities and Arts subjects.

Table 2.1 National curriculum subjects

Primary	Secondary
English	English (KS3 and 4)
Mathematics	Citizenship (KS3 and 4)
Science	Information and Communication Technology (KS3 and 4)
Information and Communication Technology	Mathematics (KS3 and 4)
	Physical Education (KS3 and 4)
Geography	Science (KS3 and 4)
History	Religious Education (KS3 and 4)
Art and Design	Art and Design (KS3 only)
Music	Modern Foreign Languages (KS3 only)
Physical Education	Design and Technology (KS3 only)
Design and Technology	History (KS3 only)
Religious Education	Geography (KS3 only)

With the exception of Religious Education, which is planned locally, each subject is broken down into programmes of study for each key stage and lists the knowledge, skills and understanding which is expected of each pupil in different areas. For example, in primary Science, learning is divided into four areas: scientific enquiry; life processes and living things; materials and their properties; and physical processes. These areas then have headings about what should be taught at each key stage. The DFES' Standards Site gives schemes of work for each subject area to support planning.

brilliant example

In Year 6, pupils in Science are learning about interdependence and adaption, which is the relationship between plants and animals and their environment. They follow the programme of study as defined by the national curriculum and also the scheme of work which is available on the DFES' Standards Site: www.standards.dfes.gov.uk (look under subject list and then Science at Key Stage 2).

Look at the site to see how many hours should be allocated to this topic and how the lessons will progress. How useful do you think this will be as a resource?

The Early Years Foundation Stage/Early Years Framework

Depending on the country of the UK you live in, the curriculum for the Early Years may be given a different heading or title and may extend to a different age. The Early Years Foundation Stage (EYFS) is the framework which is used in nursery and reception classes and in childcare settings for children up to five years in England. In Wales the Early Years Framework is also known as the Foundation Phase and extends up to seven years. In Scotland and Northern Ireland there are also separate curricula which focus on the needs of pupils who are at the earlier stages of learning. In Scotland, the curriculum is focused around the document, *A Curriculum for Excellence: Building the Curriculum 3–18*. The curriculum for three- to five-year-olds and the early primary phase (Primary 1) are presented as one level. This means that, although in Scotland there is a distinction between the phases, children only start to have more formal teaching when they are ready. There is also a strong emphasis on active learning and on deepening pupils' knowledge.

The Early Years curriculum is distinct from the rest of the curriculum in England and Wales in that it is divided into six areas of learning, which are:

- communication, language and literacy;
- problem solving, reasoning and numeracy;
- knowledge and understanding of the world;
- personal, social and emotional development;
- creative development;
- physical development.

These six areas of learning broadly cover other curriculum subjects which children will study from Key Stage 1 onwards: for example, ICT and Science will be incorporated under knowledge and understanding of the world, and Art and Music under creative development. The areas of learning will also be further divided: for example, communication, language and literacy is broken down into language for communication, language for thinking, linking sounds and letters, reading, writing and handwriting. Under each of these headings there will then be early learning goals which set out the expected end of stage level of attainment before children go into Year 1 (for planning in the Early Years see page 29).

The way in which learning is usually managed in the Early Years is that adults work alongside children on focused activities that involve specific concepts, such as using numbers or the development of writing or language activities. Children also work independently and self-select from a wide range of activities within and outside the classroom which encourage them to develop their autonomy and independence whilst developing their knowledge and skills. These will include activities such as messy play, sensory activities, cutting and sticking, painting, use of writing corner, role play, sand and water and so on.

At this stage of learning you will also be supporting pupils as they settle into school. Although not part of the curriculum, it is

> it is important that this transition phase is managed well

important that this transition phase is managed well so that children feel confident and secure in their new environment. You will need to be able to do the following:

- encourage and promote children's independence;
- take time to talk to children and get to know them individually;
- make sure that activities take account of children's needs;
- gradually integrate them into the life of the school.

(See also Chapter 8 on providing pastoral support to pupils.)

If you are working with this age group in school and have not done so before, you should have some additional advice and support through your school as there are differences in the way the Early Years curriculum is planned and assessed and it is less formal than the curriculum in other year groups. At the time of writing, the Early Years curriculum is again undergoing a period of change so you will need to make sure you are up to date with the latest developments. You will particularly need to know and understand the way in which observations are carried out and lead into planning, and also how planning is based on the interests of the children.

brilliant case study

Lulu is working in a small one-form entry primary school and usually floats between Years 1 and 2. The teaching assistant who has worked in the reception class for the last few years has gone on maternity leave and, as cover is needed, Lulu has been asked to step in for a few months. She does not have experience of the EYFS and soon starts to feel that she needs more support from her school.

- Where should Lulu go for support in the first instance?
- Is there anywhere else Lulu could seek help?

brilliant tip

If you are working with this age group, make sure you have seen a copy of the practice guidance for the Early Years curriculum in your home country. This will give you clear guidelines for what is expected of pupils and how they should be assessed.

Timetables

The way in which teachers plan their timetables at the Early Years stage will depend on the structure of the school day. For example, the timings of breaks, lunchtimes and assemblies, as well as the use of rooms such as halls and outside areas may depend on when they are being used by other classes or depend on routines and staffing. Usually, children of this age do not have playtimes and assemblies with the rest of the school, particularly when they are very new to the school environment. Foundation Stage classes will have their own outside area and the way in which their day is structured will be different, so this should not be necessary in any case. It is important for young children to have set routines although these will still need to be flexible due to the needs of this age group.

brilliant case study

Tina has just got a job supporting a reception teacher working in a small school. In her first job as a teaching assistant, she was at a larger primary where the reception and nursery classes worked together as a unit for ▶

the Foundation Stage and did not have much contact with the rest of the school, particularly as they were housed in a separate building. In her new job, the school does not have a nursery, and the reception class are expected to join in far more with whole school activities such as assemblies. Tina is surprised by the difference and is quite unsettled as a result as she is not sure that it is appropriate for this age group.

● Do you think that this could be a problem?

● Should Tina say anything?

Timetabling for older pupils will follow a more familiar structure and will usually be taught by subject, although where there are opportunities these may well overlap (for example, if pupils are working on graphs on the computers as part of their Mathematics). The way in which you support learners may vary according to timetable, and present different challenges, particularly in secondary schools where you may have to get from one end of the school to another between lessons, or have fewer opportunities to meet with teachers.

the way you support learners may vary according to timetable

In special schools, timetables may be specific to individual pupils rather than classes but this will depend on the type of school and the needs of the children.

Planning

As you are working with teachers on a daily basis it is useful to understand the way in which planning takes place and how these plans fit together. Although formats may be different from school to school, the basics are likely to be the same. Plans are usually written some time in advance, and will at the earliest stages take the form of long-, medium- and finally short-term plans (see Table 2.2).

Table 2.2 Planning stages

Stage of planning	Purpose	Content
Long term (curriculum framework)	Shows coverage of subject and provides breadth	Summary of subject content
Medium term (termly or half termly)	Provides a framework for all subjects	Shows overview of activities and/or topics. Links to national strategies
Short term	Provides a plan for the week's lessons which can be broken down by day	Should include: • learning intentions • activities • organisation/differentiation • provision for SEN • use of other adults • rough time allocations • space for notes

- Long-term plans: these are usually for the whole year – they may also be called schemes of work.

- Medium-term plans: these are for the term or half term and set out the progression within each plan.

- Short-term plans: these are for the week or day and will incorporate learning objectives and state how the class or group will be organised.

It could be that the teacher plans for the long and medium term, and that you are involved in short-term or daily plans, or plans for individual sessions. Ideally you and the teacher should plan together so that you are clear from the outset what you will be doing and are given the opportunity to put forward your own ideas. In the case of teaching assistants who support individual pupils, this can be particularly beneficial since they will be able to identify any difficulties with planned activities at the earliest stages and will also know in advance if they will need to find particular resources.

> you and the teacher should plan together

Plans should not be a secret and creating them is part of the teacher's role; if it is difficult for you to see them in advance and this is a problem, keep trying to find out how it may be possible for you to see them before the lesson. You and the teacher are both there to support pupil learning – neither of you can do your job effectively if you have no time to communicate with one another.

brilliant tip

If you do not have time to plan with teachers, ask them to email plans to you when they are completed so that you are able to look through them before the lesson.

Whatever plan you are following or lesson you are supporting, you should know the learning objectives so that you and the pupils are clear about what they will be expected to have achieved by the end of the session. This is true of pupils of any age; for example, if you are working with Early Years children you can still tell them verbally 'Today we are learning to ...', whilst with older pupils the learning objectives should be displayed and discussed at the start of each lesson. If pupils are not informed about the purpose of their learning they are less likely to be engaged in the lesson. In addition, many schools now use Assessment for Learning as a means of encouraging pupils to be part of the assessment process (for more on this see Chapter 3). This has become a regularly used motivational way of encouraging pupils of all ages to take responsibility for their own learning. It is a way of ensuring that learners are clear on the purpose of what they are doing, what they need to do and how close they are to achieving it.

brilliant example: an RE lesson plan for Year 5

Learning objective: I know some of the key facts about Judaism and Sukkot

- In small groups on large paper the children should brainstorm everything they know about Jews, Judaism, being Jewish, share as a class – what questions would you ask a Jewish person visiting our school?

- Groups to share ideas with the class: make a list of appropriate vocabulary on the board

- Tell children over the next few weeks we will be learning about Sukkot, a Jewish festival. Tell children why it is celebrated. Give children the 'key facts' sheet on Sukkot, ask them to make notes as you talk it through. TA to support blue table with this.

- Assessment for Learning opportunity – go through what they have learned about Sukkot – peer assess – do their notes reflect this?

Keep their large sheets of paper so that we can compare their knowledge at the end of the unit.

At the Early Years level, plans may take the form of topic-based ideas so that learning can be linked to a particular theme. For example, the popular topic of transport in reception classes can encompass each of the six areas of learning. Figure 2.1 overleaf shows how it may be related to each. (For more on planning and assessment see Chapter 3.)

brilliant dos and don'ts

Do

✔ Get involved with planning as much as you can.

Knowledge and understanding of the world

- Rolling vehicles down a ramp – which will go the furthest?
- Remote-controlled car/Bee-Bots to describe direction and use positional language.
- Find the road you live on using a simplified local map.
- Make a ferry for the water tray.

Communication, language and literacy

- Transport songs and rhymes – 'Wheels on the Bus', 'The Big Ship Sails', 'Row, Row, Row Your Boat', 'A Sailor Went to Sea', 'This is the Way We Cross the Road', etc.
- Any stories or books about transport.
- Describe a vehicle to children and ask them to identify it.
- Drawing letter shapes in the sand using cars.
- Put your hand in the feely bag and describe the vehicle.

Problem solving, reasoning and numeracy

- Ordering different vehicles by size.
- Sorting vehicles into colours, numbers of wheels, etc.
- Problem solving – how many people can you fit into the bus?
- Picture graph showing types of transport children have used/how they travel to school.

Transport

Creative development

- Paint/draw/make a vehicle using different media.
- Role play area – airport, inside a bus or a car, a petrol station.
- Paint tracks using tyres of different sizes.

Physical development

- Variety of ride-on vehicles in outdoor area.
- Car wash for vehicles.
- Vehicles in sand/diggers in gravel.
- Large tyres in outside area.
- Making vehicles from dough/tracks in dough using toys.

Personal, social and emotional development

- How many of these vehicles have you travelled in? Where would you be going to use them?
- Talk about journeys children have taken.
- Visit by a road safety officer.
- Working co-operatively to build a vehicle using construction/junk materials.

Figure 2.1 An example of a plan for reception with the theme of transport

✔ Ask to see any long-term plans as these will need to be done well in advance.

✔ Contribute to planning in your own way by putting forward suggestions of your own, particularly if you support an individual pupil.

✔ Check that you understand plans if anything is not clear to you.

Don't

✘ Criticise plans – if you have suggestions make them sensitively.

✘ Try to change plans unless you have been asked to do so.

✘ Worry if pupils finish activities in advance – but have something else up your sleeve if they do!

brilliant case study

Alistair is an experienced teaching assistant who is working with a newly qualified teacher in Year 5. They have been working well throughout the autumn term and the teacher sends Alistair her plans each week in advance. However, on looking through the Maths plans for the following week, Alistair has noticed that she is aiming to deliver an ambitious lesson to the group which he knows that some of the pupils he supports are going to struggle with.

● Should Alistair say something and, if so, what?

● How can this situation be managed sensitively if these kinds of issues continue?

Subject specialisms

As the role of the teaching assistant has developed, in some secondary schools there have also been developments in the way in which staff are allocated in different departments. If you have a particular strength in a subject you may be asked to stay within that subject area so that you can support teaching and learning more effectively. You will also be able to develop your own knowledge of the subject and work more closely on planning as there will be fewer time constraints. This has benefits for pupils as you will get to know the curriculum in your subject as well as the plans which are delivered by teachers.

brilliant example

Finley works in the IT department of a secondary school. He is a graduate in ICT and has taken a teaching assistant job at the school as he is interested in pursuing a career as a teacher. He has been able to work closely with the department and has supported ICT teachers in updating the school's website as well as supporting teaching and learning within the school.

You may also, however, be asked to work in a specific curriculum area if this is dictated by the needs of the school. In this case you may need to develop your own subject knowledge. If you need to do this, a good starting point will be to think about your knowledge and skills in relation to the curriculum that you are supporting. You can do this in different ways:

> think about your knowledge and skills

- Identify your knowledge of the curriculum area.
- Think about transferable skills which you may be able to bring to the subject.
- Speak to teachers about expectations within the curriculum area and sit in on lessons.

- Speak to or work alongside other teaching assistants who have supported the subject.

- Seek advice and support through your own continuing professional development (CPD).

 brilliant case study

Sinem has been asked to work within the Biology department at her school as there are not enough support staff for this area. Although she has studied the subject at school herself, that was a long time ago and she does not feel confident enough to support pupils in Biology. She usually works in the Geography and PE departments.

- What might be a good starting point for Sinem?

- How could she use support available within the school and beyond to support her knowledge and skills?

In either case you will need to work with teachers to ensure that you contribute to planning, delivery and evaluation of lessons wherever possible. If you are employed by the school to support an individual pupil you will need to stay with them to assist with all curriculum subjects, depending on the amount of hours support they have.

brilliant recap

- Be clear on the curriculum requirements for the age and stage of the pupils you are supporting.

- If you cannot see or talk about plans in advance, discuss other ways of finding out.

- Make sure you know learning objectives and finer details of the plan.

▶

- Find out about how colleagues in other schools are involved in planning.
- Support the school curriculum using your own areas of expertise.

Further reading

- www.standards.dfes.gov.uk – Standards Site for schemes of work.
- www.nc.uk.net – National curriculum.
- www.scotland.gov.uk – Scottish curriculum.
- www.deni.gov.uk – Northern Ireland curriculum.

CHAPTER 3

Supporting
teaching
and learning
– making
an effective
contribution

All teaching assistants will be required to support teaching and learning in some way as this is the main focus of their role. However, you may be asked to support individuals, groups or even whole classes, depending on your experience and knowledge. It is also likely that at some stage you will be asked to support pupil learning outside the classroom, for example on school visits, outdoor activities or as part of extended school provision. At all times you will need to encourage independent learning through being an enabler to pupils and to support their understanding – remember you are not there to carry out the task for them! If you need to give pupils too much support, they are not able to manage the task and you should refer to the class teacher.

> you are not there to carry out the task for them!

When you start in a new role you should always find out if you will be expected to cover whole classes – policies vary between local authorities but in most cases you should not be asked to do this unless you are an HLTA or have been specifically trained as a cover supervisor. You will need to have a good understanding of what you are expected to do and make sure that you are working towards clear learning objectives and that pupils are also aware of them. Even from the earliest stages it is useful to talk to pupils about what they are trying to find out and why they are working on a particular task or in a particular way.

Planning

Even if you do not have time to plan with teachers individually – although some assistants do – you should try to find out in advance what you will be expected to work on with pupils. This may be a challenge depending on the relationship you have with teachers and how regularly you are able to speak to them. If at all possible you should ask to see a lesson plan so that you are best prepared to support pupils – in some classrooms you will find that these are displayed on the wall. If you are unable to see plans it is important that you find out the following before a lesson:

- The learning objective (or what pupils are expected to be able to do at the end of the lesson).
- Who you are going to be working with.
- Any resources that you are expected to use and how to use them.

If you do not have this information before walking into the class, it will mean that you are not making full use of your time as a support to both teacher and pupils (for more on planning see Chapter 2).

Supporting different learning styles

An important thing to remember when supporting pupil learning is that everyone learns differently. Older pupils or adults may be aware that they learn best when they are listening to music or writing everything down, or that they won't be able to settle down to work unless they have been for a jog beforehand! However, younger pupils may learn best in a more practical way. Learning styles is the term given to the way that individuals learn – Howard Gardner wrote in 1983 that we each possess a particular learning style which comes under one

> everyone learns differently

of eight general headings. These in turn will influence how we learn, and how we work best:

- Verbal/linguistic – these people learn best by reading and writing.
- Logical/mathematical – these people learn best through logical activities and have a good numerical ability.
- Musical – these individuals respond best through auditory activities and are sensitive to sounds and music.
- Body/physical – these people learn best when they are moving or doing something physical.
- Visual/spatial – these people work well when they are able to visualise and use spatial judgement.
- Naturalistic – these learners respond best to natural surroundings.
- Interpersonal – these people tend to be extroverts and enjoy interacting and communicating with others.
- Intrapersonal – these people tend to be introverted and work best on their own.

Although Howard Gardner's learning styles are now sometimes considered superfluous, as it is widely acknowledged that most of us possess a range of learning styles. Whatever age you are supporting, it is important that different ways of learning are acknowledged and planned for. It is also important that lessons are not all about sitting still and listening to an adult – there is a limit to how much information can be absorbed unless the learner is actively engaged in the learning process. It is helpful to think about three main styles which are visual, auditory and kinaesthetic.

- **Visual learners** learn best through looking, seeing and reading.
- **Auditory learners** learn best through speaking and listening.

- **Kinaesthetic learners** need to be able to learn in a 'hands on' way, for example through taking on information in a more practical way.

↗ brilliant case study

Delainey, Billy and Marisa are in the same Year 2 group for Maths. You have been asked to work with them on an activity to check their knowledge and understanding of place value. Delainey learns by looking and following instructions; Billy enjoys trying things out and having a go; Marisa listens carefully and likes to discuss what she is doing as she works.

- How do you think you might better help them by thinking about different learning styles?
- Can you think of an example of how you might take them through the activity?

Using praise

Whenever you are supporting learning, and at whatever age, you should not underestimate the power of praise. Pupils will always respond positively to encouragement and recognition for the task they are undertaking. It is likely that you will do this anyway without thinking about it, but it is important to be aware of its impact on pupil learning: verbal praise in particular can be very powerful. Your school may also have a system for giving out stickers, stamps or team points to pupils depending on their age. However, you should check which of these are used where you are working as you will need to make sure that it is school policy.

> you should not underestimate the power of praise

case study

Ellie is supporting in Year 1 and has recently started working in a new school. She is an experienced assistant and has always kept stickers in her pocket to hand out to pupils. During a Maths lesson she notices that one girl is trying particularly hard and gives her a sticker. Later on the class teacher tells Ellie that stickers are never used in that particular school and that verbal praise is seen as far more powerful. Ellie is very surprised.

- What do you think about Ellie's reaction?
- Is anyone in the wrong here?
- What else could Ellie do the next time she sees the girl trying hard?

Feeding back to teachers

Although everyone in schools always seems to be extremely busy, you should make sure that you always give feedback to teachers about your work with pupils. Some teachers and teaching assistants do this as a matter of course, but in some schools it is harder than others to find time, and secondary school staff in particular can find it very difficult due to the way in which the curriculum and timetable is structured. Although it can be quicker to give verbal feedback to teachers, this can sometimes be 'lost' in the course of a busy day. Some assistants might jot down notes and give them to teachers at the end of the session, particularly if the pupil or pupils with whom they are working have found the task very difficult or too easy. It is sometimes also helpful to write down specific phrases or vocabulary which a pupil has used. In some schools it is the policy to complete more formal feedback sheets which will give a clear breakdown of each pupil's response, whilst in others teachers may ask you to mark pupils' work and leave comments such as 'Supported by TA' with a breakdown of how pupils managed the task (an example of a feedback form is given in Appendix 2).

Factors affecting pupil learning

You may well find that whilst you are working with pupils that you regularly come up against difficulties – this is bound to happen and will affect the most experienced practitioners! The kinds of problems you may face will vary (see Figure 3.1) and the more experienced you become the more likely it is that you will see them coming – sometimes before they have happened – and are able to avoid them. The important thing is to remember

Figure 3.1 Children's learning has many different influences
Source: Burnham, L. (2007) *S/NVQ Level 3 The Teaching Assistant's Handbook: Primary School*

that your response will make a difference to how this resolves itself – or doesn't.

Problems you may encounter include the following.

Intelligence and creativity

Pupils will always have different levels of ability and will have skills in different areas. They may also feel that they are not able to achieve in a particular area, for example in writing or Maths, or in more creative subjects such as Art or Music. This may affect their motivation and what they are able to do. You should always try to encourage them to try new things and to take risks with their learning.

> encourage them to try new things

Age and maturity

Pupils will develop at their own pace and learning will occur at different rates in different children, though there will be an average age at which children achieve various milestones. Remember also that in any one class there will be a spread of ages – some may be born in September whilst others may not have their birthdays until the end of the academic year. At the earliest stages of schooling this may well make quite a difference and it may be worth finding out about children's birthdays.

Gender

Some pupils may come from a background which gives them more or fewer learning opportunities due to their gender. For example, a boy might be given more academic encouragement than his sister due to family expectations. As school staff it is important that we do not discriminate on the basis of gender, for example, by only allowing girls to do cooking activities, or only boys to do football.

Physical factors

There are a number of reasons why physical factors might affect learning. Depending on their age and maturity, some pupils may have less control over their fine and gross motor skills which might impact on their ability to carry out a task. Fine motor skills are skills such as holding a pencil or using a knife and fork effectively, while gross motor skills are skills such as running, jumping, skipping and whole body movements. Also, if pupils have special educational needs such as a visual impairment, this might mean that they need more support in order to access the curriculum. Depending on the environment, you may find that the area you are working in has been booked by someone else, there is insufficient space for the number of pupils, or is too hot, too cold or too noisy. Always check the area first if at all possible. If you have been unable to do this beforehand and it turns out to be unsuitable, you will need to find an alternative to ensure that the pupils are able to benefit from the activity. There is no point in attempting to work there if, for example, there is a lot of noise immediately outside the room, or if the temperature in the room is not conducive to learning.

always check the area first if at all possible

Ability to remain on task

Pupils of different ages will vary in their ability to concentrate on a task – broadly speaking, the younger the child, the shorter the concentration span. They may also look for more reassurance from adults and those around them. As pupils become older, most will be able to concentrate for a set time without becoming distracted. At any stage, if one or a group of pupils' ability to concentrate is very different from that of their classmates, this may affect the learning of others.

Linguistic factors

Language is the key element to pupil learning. If pupils have problems such as a speech and language disorder or have not been encouraged to socialise with others, they may find learning more challenging. This is because language is the route through which we begin to learn to rationalise our thoughts in an abstract way. We need to encourage the development of language as much as possible in children from the earliest stage so that they are given as much opportunity as possible to develop their confidence and vocabulary. As well as speaking to pupils as much as possible during learning activities, we must also encourage discussion and a wide range of stories and first-hand experiences. Pupils who speak English as an additional language can also find it harder to learn if they are not supported effectively (see Chapter 6). In more extreme cases, those who have limited language may also have behavioural difficulties if they are unable to vocalise their feelings, which can in turn lead to frustration.

Emotional factors

Pupils will naturally be affected by their home background and whether this is happy and settled. There can be a huge number of reasons why this is not the case, such as bereavement, separated parents or new parental partners, alcoholism in the family and so on. Pupils may also become upset about things which may seem insignificant to an adult, such as being unable to say goodbye to a parent that day or an argument with a sibling. In cases like this you may need to take the pupil aside and speak to them about what is upsetting them so that you are able to continue. If they are too upset to work you will be unable to make them do so.

Social, cultural and ethnic background

All pupils will be affected by their background and whether they have had positive social experiences. This will affect their learning, for example, if they have had limited experience of meeting others, which may in turn give them less confidence. In areas of social deprivation you may find that pupils have come to school without eating, or without enough clothes. These kinds of issues will also affect their ability to learn. Depending on pupils' culture or ethnicity they may have learned to do things in a particular way which may not be in keeping with that of the school. Remember, if you have reason to be concerned about a pupil you should refer this to a member of teaching staff.

all pupils will be affected by their background

Motivation

We all know what it feels like to be motivated by something and pupils are no different. Motivation will clearly affect their learning as it is the interest which they have in a task. If a pupil does not see a purpose to what they are doing, the task is unclear or they are unable to do it, they will quickly become demotivated. It is important that any adults working with the child ensure that they are able to carry out the task and that it makes sense to them.

Problems with resources

You should make sure in advance that you have sufficient resources, particularly if they are slightly different from the usual. Even if the teacher has set up for you it is still worth checking to make sure you have enough of everything. If you are working with pupils who have additional needs you will need to make sure that all the resources are appropriate for them and that they will be able to access the curriculum as much as the other pupils. Remember that if you are working with technology such as computers you should always have alternative plans if for some reason they don't work!

brilliant tip

When working with pupils on learning activities, regularly stop and ask yourself 'What do I want the pupils to learn?' and reiterate the learning objective. This can help you to refocus pupils on the task.

Supporting individuals

There may be a number of reasons you are supporting an individual pupil. The first is that you have been specifically employed to support them in the classroom because they have a statement of special educational needs. However, if you support different classes or are based in learning support you may also work periodically with pupils who have specific learning needs such as dyslexia. If you are working with an individual pupil you should make sure you know something about them before you start – even if this is something about their interests or talents. This will be invaluable to you whilst you are supporting teaching and learning. This is because it may help you to draw them out and develop a relationship with them. If you are employed to work one-to-one with a pupil you will also need to find out as much as you can about their needs and individual educational targets on paperwork such as Individual Education Plans (IEPs) and Personal Support Plans (PSPs). You should speak to your school's SENCO or inclusion manager to clarify how you should work on specific targets and how much time you will need to work alone with them, or whether you should support them as part of a group. Remember to always speak to teachers if you are not clear about your role when supporting individual pupils.

Supporting groups

Most teaching assistants will work with groups on a regular basis. This may be as part of an intervention programme within the school which you are involved with, or simply as part of your work within the classroom. If you have been asked to work with a group, it may sound obvious but you should remember to involve *all* pupils – it is easy to just focus your questioning on those who are eager to answer. Quieter pupils will often benefit from working in small groups as it will help their confidence, so try to draw them in wherever possible. Look out for those who are losing concentration as they may start to distract others or gain attention in a negative way. You may also have been given a group who do not work well together – do not be afraid of speaking to the teacher about it if the group does not 'gel'.

> remember to involve *all* pupils

Supporting whole classes

You may be asked to cover whole classes as part of your role in a mainstream school. If you have had specific training or are very experienced you may be equipped to do this. However, you should make sure that you are covered by insurance (for example, you should not take PE lessons unless you have specific training) and know what you are expected to cover, as teachers should draw up a plan for you.

Teaching assistants are also sometimes asked to cover for planning, preparation and assessment (PPA) time for teachers, and this has been the subject of discussion in the educational press. There is no legal reason why you should not take whole classes as some teaching assistants are very experienced and qualified. However, if you are uncomfortable or do not feel experienced enough to do it you should say so. If you are unhappy with what you are being asked to do you should check your contract and job description to see whether it includes any mention of cover under your duties.

Cover supervision

Cover supervisors are most often found in secondary schools but can also be found in primary and special schools. They may be asked to take lessons on a regular basis and cover for staff absence although they should not be asked to plan lessons themselves. If you are a cover supervisor you should have advance warning that you are going to take a class so that you are able to discuss plans with teachers, or at least be left detailed plans. You should not be asked to plan and mark work for teachers.

brilliant tip

When working with groups or whole classes, agree ground rules with them during your first session and talk to them about what will happen if these are not met. This will make it clear what is acceptable to the group and what is not. It is far easier to manage pupils if they are aware of the boundaries and agree rules together. You should always make sure that these are phrased positively, for example, 'always show respect to others' rather than focusing on the negative of 'don't do this', and make expectations clear.

Monitoring and modifying activities whilst you are working with pupils

It is likely that at some stage you will need to modify the work that pupils are carrying out with you – this is completely normal, but you need to be ready for it. An example might be if you are working with a group and some pupils finish their work before others: you may need to give them additional work to do (often called an extension activity). You should check with the teacher whether you need to do this and if they have something in mind *before* you start working with the group. It is also possible that a pupil is working much faster or much slower than the rest of the group. In this situation you should speak to the pupil and ask them to check their work before moving on to the next activity.

When to refer to others

You may find that while you are working with pupils you need to refer back to the teacher. This could be for a number of reasons, although you should make sure that you have done what you can first. You will need to be sensitive when doing this, particularly if the teacher is occupied with other pupils – make sure you choose your moment carefully!

> make sure you choose your moment carefully!

Reasons may include:

- pupil behaviour;
- activity is too hard or too easy for pupils;
- a pupil who has special educational needs is unable to access the task.

If you are unable to speak to the teacher for the time being, make sure you give pupils an alternative activity or, in cases of poor behaviour, separate them from one another.

brilliant dos and don'ts

Do

✔ Make sure you are ready and fully prepared each time you support pupils.

✔ Make sure you have seen plans and know the learning objectives.

✔ Use your initiative if you spot something that needs doing.

✔ Make sure you feed back to the teacher afterwards, even if this is through handwritten notes and feedback sheets.

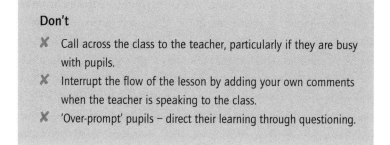

Don't

✗   Call across the class to the teacher, particularly if they are busy with pupils.

✗   Interrupt the flow of the lesson by adding your own comments when the teacher is speaking to the class.

✗   'Over-prompt' pupils – direct their learning through questioning.

Carrying out pupil assessments and observations

You should be carrying out assessments on pupils all the time as part of the work you do in supporting teaching and learning in schools. Teachers have to monitor and assess pupil achievement throughout the academic year and your role is to support them in doing this so that they can feed back to headteachers.

Types of assessment

Assessment may take different forms.

Formative assessment

This is everyday assessment which takes place through observations, questioning, and talking to pupils to check their understanding. You should always monitor what pupils say to you whilst carrying out learning activities, as this will enable you to do this.

Summative assessment

This is used to check learning at the end of a topic, year, or scheme of work so that teachers can recap and assess how much pupils have achieved. It could be that this takes the form of SATs, or end of year tests prior to writing school reports.

Assessment for Learning (AfL)

This is increasingly used by schools to monitor pupil learning using peer- and self-assessment. Assessment for Learning informs and promotes the achievement of all pupils as it encourages them to take responsibility for their own learning. The process involves explaining learning outcomes to pupils, giving them feedback on their progress and enabling them to develop their self-assessment skills so that they are ultimately able to reflect on and recognise their own achievements. This will usually start with pupils taking part in peer-assessment to build up these skills and discuss their work before moving on to thinking about their own work. Pupils will need to be able to carefully consider their learning throughout the process and keep coming back to the learning objective or what they are expected to learn. At the end of the session they will then revisit the objective and decide whether they have been successful.

Benefits for teachers

Effective Assessment for Learning will enable the teacher to pass on the responsibility to the child over time for managing their own learning so that they will become more actively involved in the process.

Benefits for pupils

The process will inform pupils about how they approach learning and tackle areas on which they need to work. They will be able to consider areas for improvement by looking at assessment criteria and develop their ability to self-assess. Their increased awareness of how to learn will develop their confidence and help them to recognise when to ask for support.

Benefits for you

Assessment for Learning will inform how you approach pupil questioning based on what you have discovered about how they learn. You may need to pace the progress of learners depending on their needs so that less able pupils are given opportunities to revisit areas of uncertainty.

For more on Assessment for Learning, see page 119.

brilliant tip

If your school uses Assessment for Learning ask whether you can observe it in progress. If there is whole school training on AfL, support staff should also be able to attend.

Observations

Although you will be observing pupils all the time, you may be asked to carry out specific observations without working directly with a pupil. The reasons for this may be:

- to observe how the pupil interacts with others;
- to observe as part of the Early Years Foundation Stage;
- to monitor a pupil's special educational need;
- to monitor behaviour.

When carrying out observations, check with the teacher how you should record the information, whether there is a specific format and how much detail is required. For example, when carrying out Early Years observations the main criteria may be that they are timed (two to three minutes) and should include a large amount of detail.

brilliant recap

- Be prepared for all eventualities!
- Remember the importance of planning and feedback.
- Be aware that you are observing and assessing pupils at all times.
- Remember the power of praise.

CHAPTER 4

Managing behaviour

Since the introduction of workforce remodelling in 2003, which set out to clarify the roles of teachers and support staff, there has been an increase in the number of different professionals working in schools, all of whom will need to know how to manage pupils' behaviour effectively. The whole school team will need to be able to understand and implement agreed classroom management strategies alongside colleagues as part of a consistent approach to encourage positive behaviour.

Behaviour management will take place in a variety of contexts, including round the school, during lunchtimes, on school trips and in different learning environments. You should be able to show that you are aware of your school's behaviour policy and are part of this approach to managing behaviour. You should also be able to encourage pupils to take responsibility for their own behaviour within the framework of the school code of conduct and through being part of the wider school community.

The importance of an agreed code of conduct

When pupils first come into a school environment they will need to learn to comply with the school's expectations for behaviour. This may be different from parental expectations – what is acceptable at home may not be acceptable in the school environment or in wider society. All schools will need to have an agreed code of conduct which pupils know and refer to

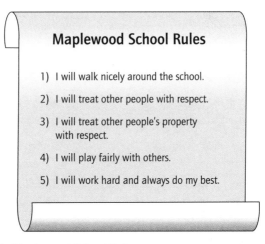

Figure 4.1 Maplewood School Rules

regularly. This is important so that pupils know what is expected of them and are aware of consequences before they act rather than afterwards. Behaviour needs to be managed proactively, that is so that all pupils are aware of expectations and conse-

quences – in this way they will be able to take responsibility for their own behaviour. Although all schools will have 'school rules' (Figure 4.1) it is also likely that individual classes

> behaviour needs to be managed proactively

or subjects will also have their own agreed codes of conduct – for example in a Chemistry lab or an ICT suite. It is helpful if pupils can be involved in devising these rules to draw attention to them and also so that they have more ownership of them.

brilliant case study

Year 2 have been in the class for almost half a term and the class teacher and teaching assistant have devised an agreed set of rules with the children which are displayed on the wall. Ralf has recently started to be spiteful to another child in the class and has said that he does not want to play with him or be his friend. The class teacher says to him, 'Ralf, we agreed as a class that we will always be kind to others.'

- Do you think that Ralf will be more likely to listen to the teacher since he helped devise the rules?
- What else could staff do to try to ensure that this kind of behaviour occurs less frequently?

Working in groups

Pupils will also need to work with adults in groups, sometimes for a series of lessons or on intervention work. If you are the supporting adult in this situation you should always speak to pupils before starting the first session about what kinds of group rules you should have, and record them so that they are available for future sessions. In this way you are making the pupils aware of your expectations, as well as those of their peers. If you find that you have a particular pupil or pupils who are disrupting the rest of the group you will need to apply sanctions straight away so that this does not become the norm each time you take the group.

School policy for rewards and sanctions

Your school's behaviour policy should set out the rewards and sanctions which are available to you to use as a member of staff. It is important that all adults have read and/or had training on the expectations and responsibilities of staff when managing behaviour. This may need to be updated regularly so that all new staff are also aware of the school's policy. If you have any worries or concerns about how to deal with specific behaviour you should always refer to a teacher or your school SENCO.

Depending upon the age and/or needs of pupils, your rewards and sanctions may be very different – this is to ensure that they are age appropriate. Pupils in a secondary school, for example, will probably not be as fazed by having their name put on the board as younger pupils – in a similar way, very young pupils will be unlikely to be given a detention! Your school should have a scale of sanctions for you to use with pupils when behaviour is inappropriate. This structured approach should be very clear so that the consequences are listed in order, for example:

> rewards and sanctions may be very different

1   Time out.

2   Miss one minute or longer of playtime.

3   Be sent to the deputy head or the headteacher.

4   Teacher speaks to parents.

You should also check to see what particular rewards are given to pupils for effort and behaviour – this might take the form of merit marks, team points, stickers, certificates and so on. It is unlikely that as a teaching assistant you will be unable to apply particular sanctions or rewards but you should check – in case, for example, only teachers can give detentions.

brilliant activity

Using a copy of your school's behaviour policy, highlight or note down:

● your responsibilities under the policy;

● rewards which are used in the school (team points, stickers, etc.);

● sanctions which you can use (name on board, warnings, etc.);

● how positive behaviour is promoted.

Your school may also have additional frameworks in place to support a positive environment. An important part of the learning process encourages pupils to make choices for themselves. For example, many schools now have school councils which give some responsibility to pupils and gives them opportunities to think about and discuss whole school issues and decision making within the boundaries of the school environment.

Positive behaviour management

Positive behaviour management is a focus on the positive aspects of what a pupil is doing. An example of this might be if, when speaking to pupils, we ignore inappropriate behaviour and focus on those pupils who are doing the right thing: 'Well done, Ryan, for sitting beautifully' may make others do the same in order to gain your attention.

There are a number of different ways in which adults can promote positive behaviour in schools. This is important, particularly when staff are working with specific pupils who have behaviour problems (see also page 64). We will all dwell on and think about negative comments which are made about us and children are no different; however, research has shown that we need to be given six positive comments for every negative one in order to redress the balance. It can be much easier for us to focus on the negative aspects of a pupil's behaviour and react to it because we are annoyed, although this can often make the situation worse. Praise and positive behaviour strategies will be beneficial to pupils and schools for a number of reasons:

- They create a positive environment for staff and pupils.
- They provide motivation for pupils through positive encouragement and rewards.
- They increase pupils' self-esteem and confidence.

How can we promote positive behaviour?

Modelling correct behaviour

As adults we should always model the kind of behaviour we expect from pupils. Good role models will set an example to pupils and show them how to behave. An example of this might be when we are in assembly and chatting to other staff before it starts. If pupils see us doing this they are far less likely to do it themselves – the rule is no talking, so why are adults doing it?

Notice when pupils are trying hard

Effort is just as important as achievement – it is important to keep an eye out for occasions when a pupil is really working on their behaviour or trying hard academically, particularly if they find either of these things difficult.

Showing pupils respect

As adults we need to have good manners and show respect to others. This is very important – we need to show the same respect that we are asking pupils to show so that we can build positive relationships.

Use positive recognition

As well as using verbal praise, as a teaching assistant you should also be able to use merit marks and other rewards which celebrate good work and behaviour.

Give responsibilities to pupils

This is very effective since it reinforces the pupil's self-esteem and also encourages them to think about the positive effects of helping others.

Follow up on issues which are important

You should always follow up on issues, particularly if you have made a point of saying you will. If you see Becky behaving very well in the corridor and say that you will tell her teacher how pleased you are, you must remember to do it. If you do not, there is an implication that you do not see it as important and she may be less likely to behave well again.

Be clear on why you are rewarding the pupil

Make sure, particularly with younger pupils or those who have special educational needs, that you tell them exactly why you are praising them as they may not always understand why. You can say 'I am giving you this smiley face sticker because you worked so hard on your numbers this morning.'

You should also be very aware of your own assumptions and prejudices and avoid using them in a school context. Stereotyping pupils can limit their development just as they are starting to build their own ideas. If they hear adults making prejudicial remarks they will grow up thinking that there is no harm in that type of behaviour. The pupils who are the subject of the remarks will also be damaged further by the reinforcement of low expectations and low self-esteem. Beware of stereotyping pupils even through comments such as 'I need some sensible girls to take this message for me' – this

> beware of stereotyping pupils

may sound to boys as though only girls can be sensible. Also, never assume that pupils with special educational needs do not understand situations or are unable to complete tasks – include everyone as much as you can.

brilliant tip

When working with experienced teachers, take note of how they manage behaviour in different situations and try out some of their strategies yourself where appropriate.

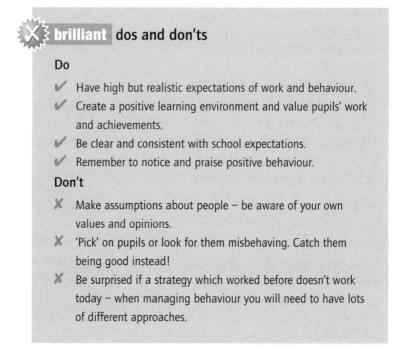

brilliant dos and don'ts

Do

✔ Have high but realistic expectations of work and behaviour.

✔ Create a positive learning environment and value pupils' work and achievements.

✔ Be clear and consistent with school expectations.

✔ Remember to notice and praise positive behaviour.

Don't

✘ Make assumptions about people – be aware of your own values and opinions.

✘ 'Pick' on pupils or look for them misbehaving. Catch them being good instead!

✘ Be surprised if a strategy which worked before doesn't work today – when managing behaviour you will need to have lots of different approaches.

Factors impacting on pupil behaviour

You should be aware that there may be a number of reasons for pupils' inappropriate or negative behaviour (see Figure 4.2). Remember also that the kind of behaviour to look out for may not just be the loud or attention-seeking kind – negative behaviour can also be passive or over-dependent. Pupils' prior domestic and social experiences will have a huge impact on the way in which they relate and react to others, and most pupils will want to gain adult attention; those who behave inappropriately may try to do this in a negative way. They will also be affected by arguments with their peers, or incidents at home. It is important to get to know pupils and to find out about

find out about their backgrounds and preferences

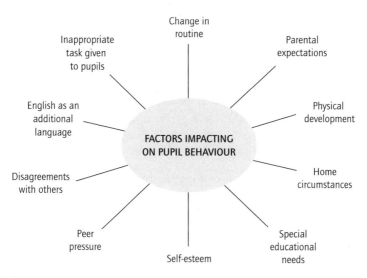

Figure 4.2 Factors impacting on pupil behaviour

their backgrounds and preferences, as this will help you to look out for behaviour which is uncharacteristic in pupils. It may also help you to understand why they may behave in a particular way. Although you may not have any control over some of these contributing factors, you should develop strategies for dealing with different situations.

Parental expectations

Parents will vary a great deal in their expectations of what is right for their child. Depending on the level of discipline which they have had growing up, the extremes may be that they are very strict or make too many allowances for their child's behaviour. Some parents may also lack confidence and ask for advice from school staff about how to manage their child's behaviour at home. These parental factors will clearly make a difference to how a pupil behaves. You may also find that pupils say to you '... but I am allowed to do that/ say that at home' when you speak to them about their behaviour. The answer to this is that we do not behave in this way in school.

Home circumstances

Pupils' backgrounds will also affect behaviour, particularly if it is unhappy. Remember that a significant number of children are victims of some form of abuse – this may be verbal, physical, sexual or through neglect. Look out for quiet and withdrawn behaviour, or pupils who seem preoccupied.

Self-esteem

Self-esteem can be high or low, positive or negative. It is how we feel about ourselves that leads to our self-image – that is, how we think about or perceive ourselves. Children develop positive self-esteem when they feel good about themselves and when they feel valued. The way in which we treat pupils will have a direct effect on this so it is important that we encourage and praise wherever we can. We must also value each child as an individual and celebrate differences and similarities.

Peer pressure

Pupils may be influenced negatively or positively by their peers. In a negative way, pressure may be put on them to conform to certain behaviour to be part of a group, particularly as they go through secondary school.

Disagreements with others

If pupils have had an argument or are upset about something which has happened at playtime, for example, they may well be affected by it during lesson time. You may find that pupils come in from break and are very quiet, or are upset in some way – never ignore this even if it means delaying what you are going to do – you should always speak to the pupils and discuss what has happened.

Special educational needs

Depending on their needs, pupils may find some aspects of learning difficult which may impact on their behaviour (see also Chapter 5 page 82).

English as an additional language

Ensure that any pupils you are supporting have an understanding of acceptable behaviour, and that if they misbehave you are clear with them why sanctions have been used. Sometimes frustration about being unable to communicate clearly with others can also cause them to behave inappropriately.

Inappropriate task given to pupils

If the task which pupils have been given to do is too easy or difficult for them, they may not be engaged in what they are doing. This may make them start to look for other things to do or distract others.

A change in routine

Sometimes this may be all that is needed to provoke unwanted behaviour in pupils. They may be excitable due to a school trip or another situation which is a change from the norm. You can anticipate this as you become more experienced and be ready for it!

Physical development

If pupils are very different physically from their peers due to, for example, different growth patterns their behaviour may be affected. They may also be treated differently by their peers due to their size. You may need to make additional provision when Year 6 are getting changed for PE, for example.

Working with individual pupils who have behavioural issues

You may, as a teaching assistant, have been employed specifically to work with a pupil who has behavioural issues. This may be caused by a number of factors or conditions. In this situation you should have clear guidance and support from your school's SENCO and from others who work with the pupil. It is likely that if they have a Statement of Special Educational Needs or are on School Action Plus there will be advice available from other agencies who have worked with the pupil. These may be:

> you should have clear guidance and support

- **Educational psychologists (EPs)**: These professionals visit schools regularly to work with and support pupils and the adults who work with them. They offer help and advice on a variety of issues and may also carry out assessments and programmes to support pupils who have special educational needs.

- **Local behaviour support teachers**: Behaviour support teachers will be based at the local education authority and can be brought in by the school to give advice and support for pupils who may have behavioural problems. They may be able to come in and work individually with pupils or to observe and offer suggestions to staff (see also Chapter 5 on supporting pupils who have special educational needs).

brilliant tip

- Intervene as soon as you can to prevent the situation from becoming worse.
- You may not need to say anything – sometimes eye contact and the right expression can prevent unwanted behaviour.

- Ignore some behaviour if possible; sometimes distraction works with younger pupils.

- Remove any items which a pupil may be using inappropriately or as a distraction.

- Relate negative comments to the behaviour rather than the pupil ('David, that was not a sensible idea') rather than telling the pupil they are not sensible.

- Be realistic about pupil behaviour – do not sit pupils together if they usually find it hard to work productively together!

When working with pupils who have issues around behaviour, you should try to develop positive relationships with them. As a member of support staff you are well placed to spend time talking to the pupil and to find out about their needs and interests. You can also find out about the pupil through speaking to your SENCO or talking to the pupil's parents or carers, or through discussions with teachers.

Remember, however, that you will need to be mindful of confidentiality and should not take any school records or reports off site. You should also not pass on any information about pupils to those who do not have a valid reason to know it.

When working with pupils who have behavioural needs you may also be involved in drawing up Behaviour Support Plans (BSPs), Individual Education Plans (IEPs) or Personal Support Plans (PSPs) which will give targets for managing their behaviour. These documents will all follow similar formats but will include two or three targets to be worked on over the following weeks. You will then need to agree a further date to meet and review the pupil's progress. Depending on the pupil's needs, the SENCO and parents may also be present. The pupil should also always be there – even from an early age – so that they can be part of the process.

Managing challenging behaviour

At some stage all school staff will come up against behaviour which is challenging and which may in some cases be aggressive or a risk to the pupil or others. In this situation you will need to keep your wits about you. Pupils may not always be aware of risks and dangerous situations, so when speaking to them you may need to point out the consequences of what they are doing. You should also be aware of your own responsibilities – if things have already got out of hand or if you are at all concerned you should send for another member of staff straight away. You should also always seek help if:

> point out the consequences of what they are doing

- you or others are in any danger;
- pupils are behaving unpredictably or aggressively;
- pupils are not carrying out your instructions and you are not in control of the situation.

Seeking help may mean sending another pupil to go and find adult help.

brilliant activity

Look at the examples here and think about which you would be able to manage on your own and which you think you would need to refer to others:

- A playground argument between two Year 6 boys which has become aggressive.
- One of the pupils in your group is extremely quiet today and when you question her at the end of the session she starts crying and says she is being bullied.

- A pupil in reception is having a full-blown temper tantrum because her childminder has just left and has taken her favourite blanket with her.
- A Year 8 pupil has become very angry during a group session with you and has stormed out.
- A special needs child has refused to take part in an activity with you because he doesn't want to.

How would you deal with those situations you could manage on your own?

Your school's behaviour policy should also give guidelines for managing challenging behaviour. You may also need to use restraint to prevent pupils from causing injury to themselves or others, but you should be careful when doing this and again have read your school's or local guidelines – remember it should be used as a last resort.

brilliant recap

- Make sure you have read and follow your school's behaviour policy.
- Be clear on what sanctions and rewards you can apply.
- Always set up ground rules when you start working with a new group.
- Make sure you have as much information and advice as possible when working with a pupil who has behavioural issues.
- Always refer to others in situations which are potentially dangerous.

Further reading

- Dix, Paul (2009) *Taking Care of Behaviour*, Pearson.

CHAPTER 5

Working with pupils who have special educational needs

f you are working as a teaching assistant, it is likely that as part of your role you will at some stage be asked to support pupils who have special educational needs (SEN). You may do this because you are employed specifically to support an individual as a learning support assistant (more on this later), however, you may also need to work with individuals or groups who need additional adult help in order to have full access to the curriculum. In order to do this you will need to have skills in a number of areas, both in your relationships with others, such as teachers, parents and other professionals, as well as having empathy and understanding for the pupils you support. It may be that you develop a high level of responsibility, particularly if you are working with an individual, as you will get to know them and their particular needs and develop partnerships with others who support them.

> you will need to have skills in a number of areas

SEN Code of Practice

The term 'special educational need' is defined by the SEN Code of Practice 2001 as 'a learning difficulty which calls for special educational provision to be made for them'. The Code of Practice (COP) is a document which sets out clearly how the provision for pupils with special educational needs should be managed within schools and local authorities. If you are working with a pupil who has special educational needs, you should be familiar with the code and its fundamental principles, which are:

- A child with special educational needs should have their needs met.

- The special educational needs of children will normally be met in mainstream schools or settings.

- The views of the child should be sought and taken into account.

- Parents have a vital role to play in supporting their child's education.

- Children with special educational needs should be offered full access to a broad, balanced and relevant education, including an appropriate curriculum for the Foundation Stage and the National Curriculum.

These principles focus on the child or young person and identify the steps which should be taken by schools and local authorities in order to support them and their families effectively. Schools should work with pupils and parents in order to ensure that as far as possible the needs of children and young people are met in mainstream schools. Your role according to the Code of Practice is to work closely with the pupil and with parents and teaching staff in order to do this.

Under the SEN Code of Practice, there are different levels of response to pupils with additional needs in schools and Early Years settings. If you are working with a pupil who has special educational needs, their level of support will be indicated on their IEP. They are set out as:

- School or Early Years Action;
- School or Early Years Action Plus;
- Statement.

Early Years Action and Action Plus are for children who are in nursery or reception classes.

School or Early Years Action

At this stage, the teacher or parent has identified that a pupil is working at a different level from the majority of the class. The school, in consultation with the pupil and with parents, will need to form and provide an educational programme which is tailored to the specific needs of the pupil. They will also need to document what steps they are taking as a record, usually in the form of targets. Depending on the age and needs of the pupil, they will be involved in identifying and agreeing targets which are achievable. This document is known as an IEP, or Individual Education Plan (see Figure 5.1), and parents and pupils will

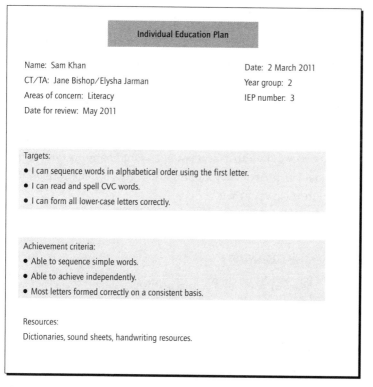

Individual Education Plan

Name: Sam Khan

CT/TA: Jane Bishop/Elysha Jarman

Areas of concern: Literacy

Date for review: May 2011

Date: 2 March 2011

Year group: 2

IEP number: 3

Targets:
- I can sequence words in alphabetical order using the first letter.
- I can read and spell CVC words.
- I can form all lower-case letters correctly.

Achievement criteria:
- Able to sequence simple words.
- Able to achieve independently.
- Most letters formed correctly on a consistent basis.

Resources:

Dictionaries, sound sheets, handwriting resources.

Figure 5.1 An example of an IEP

both need to sign a copy which they should keep, while the school copy will go in the pupil's file.

Targets

The IEP targets will have a date set for review and the school will need to make sure that this is recorded at the time of writing. Usually an IEP runs for half a term, although occasionally this may be slightly longer. If the target has not been met at the time of the review meeting, the SENCO may choose to record that it is ongoing, or amend it if it is not achievable for the pupil.

School or Early Years Action Plus

At this stage, the child or young person will have been working on their additional targets for some time. This may mean that they have had several IEPs and the school and parents may still have concerns about their progress despite the additional input. The SENCO may decide to increase the level of support to School Action Plus which means that the school will invite other professionals to assess the pupil (for examples of the kind of professionals these might be, see pages 85–7). This may happen either within or outside school, depending on their role. After the assessment, the other professional would support and advise the school on further targets and continue to help with monitoring and reviewing their progress.

↗ brilliant case study

Andre is working in Year 1 as a general teaching assistant. A child in the class, Phoebe, has shown some causes for concern due to her speech and language, which is also impacting significantly on her ability to learn. After some discussion with the SENCO and Pheobe's parents, they have decided to give her an IEP with specific language targets. Andre has been working with Phoebe three times a week for two terms on her targets but Phoebe has made little progress. After speaking to Phoebe's parents, the SENCO and class teacher decide that they will refer Phoebe to a speech and language therapist for further assessment.

● Would Phoebe now be on School Action or School Action Plus?

Statement

At the third level of intervention for pupils who have special educational needs, all professionals working with the child or young person would need to show that the school has done all it can to support them. They should then set out why they have a case for needing additional help in order to meet the needs of the pupil. This will usually be a request for a number of hours per week of individual support in the form of a teaching assistant. At this stage, the SENCO will need to gather reports from all the professionals working with the pupil as well as all of their IEPs and the views of the parents and the pupil, and put together a case which will then be considered by a panel of professionals at the local education authority which will usually meet once a month. The panel may or may not decide that the pupil needs a statutory assessment, and may ask the school for more evidence if this is not clear. If the school is successful in their request, the pupil's papers will then go to a further panel which will assess the pupil's needs. At the next stage, if successful, the pupil will be allocated a set number of hours per week of individual support. This will then be reviewed annually at a meeting with all those who work with the child to assess whether the support is still needed.

brilliant activity

Find a copy of the SEN Code of Practice 2001. Look at the 'Identification, assessment and provision' section for the age of pupil you support. How user-friendly does it seem to you?

Knowing about the needs of the pupil you support

If you are supporting a pupil who has special educational needs, you will need to know about and be able to respond to their specific needs. The Code of Practice sets out the four main areas of special educational need, and although each pupil will be different and their needs often relate to more than one area, it is helpful to have some idea of how their requirements are outlined. In each case, the needs of the pupil may be moderate, severe or profound: in other words they may be slight, or they may impact on the pupil in all that they do. The areas of need are discussed below.

> you will need to know about their specific needs

Communication and interaction

This means that the pupil may have a speech and language delay, impairment or disorder which will affect their ability to communicate with others. The causes may be due to a variety of reasons, some of which are given below.

Speech and language delays or disorders

These may range from problems such as a stutter to more complicated disorders where pupils have difficulties in thinking through their language (known as processing). Some pupils may need regular speech and language therapy in order to help them to develop their communication skills.

Autistic Spectrum Disorder (ASD)

Individuals who are autistic have a developmental disorder which affects the way in which they relate to others. This will vary in severity – whilst some pupils may just seem distracted, others may display quite disruptive behaviour such as frequent interruptions, and some may not speak at all. Autistic pupils will find it difficult to communicate with their peers and to play imaginatively, and may react inappropriately in some social situations. They may need varying degrees of support to help them to communicate effectively with others.

In addition to this, the communication abilities of pupils who have other areas of special educational need such as cognition and learning, or sensory needs, may be affected by an overriding condition. For example, a child or young person who has learning difficulties may have slower language processing skills or find it difficult to follow instructions. They might also have a limited understanding of non-verbal communication such as facial expressions or body language shown by others.

Cognition and learning

Pupils who have cognition and learning needs may find it difficult to absorb new information, and they may take longer to do their work. For effective learning to take place, pupils need to have developed a range of cognitive skills for processing and storing information. When they have difficulties in this area, there will be an impact on the development of these skills. Pupils may therefore need help in the following areas.

Language, memory and reasoning skills

Children who have cognition and learning difficulties may take longer to develop language skills. This in turn affects their learning, as they are less able to store and process information.

Sequencing and organisational skills

Pupils may need help and support when organising themselves because they may find it difficult to follow sequences of ideas.

Understanding of numbers

The abstract concepts of arithmetic may be difficult for these pupils to grasp and they will need practical help with numbers.

Problem solving and concept development
Understanding new ideas may take more time for these pupils and they may need one-to-one support.

Behaviour, social and emotional development

Pupils who have behaviour, social and emotional development needs may display challenging or immature behaviour and their needs can be varied, as the reasons for poor behaviour are complex. When managing these pupils you will need to be proactive rather than reactive in your approach – in other words, it is important that pupils are aware of guidelines for their behaviour and the consequences of their actions. They also need to be given opportunities to develop relationships with others and treat them with respect.

> be proactive rather than reactive

If you are working with these pupils as an individual support assistant you will need to work closely with other professionals to decide on the best form of intervention to use, but developing a positive relationship and finding out as much as possible about them is a good starting point. As well as their IEP, these pupils may also be given a Behaviour Support Plan (BSP) if they need to have shorter-term targets for more regular review (for more on behaviour management in general see Chapter 4). Figure 5.2 shows some intervention strategies for pupils who have social and emotional needs.

brilliant tip

What works as a great behaviour management strategy one week may not work on another – you will need to vary the strategies you use, so have plenty up your sleeve (for more on this see the further reading at the end of the chapter).

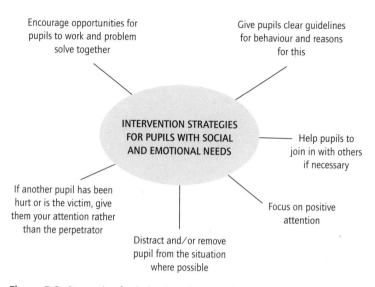

Figure 5.2 Strategies for behaviour intervention

Sensory and/or physical

Pupils with sensory and/or physical impairments will have hearing, visual or physical support needs. They may have a disability or medical condition which impacts on all areas of their learning, or they may need very little support. It should not be assumed that these pupils need any form of special educational provision if they are able to access the curriculum without support, as their condition may not impact on their educational needs. However, in some cases, pupils *will* require specialised provision to ensure that they are included in all areas of the curriculum. Depending on their needs, you should find out about any specialist equipment they have and be able to select and use any materials required to support their learning. Pupils with sensory or physical impairments may tire easily and their social and emotional development may be affected as they may become frustrated if they are not able to complete tasks as quickly or as well as they would hope to.

You should ensure that pupils with disabilities are encouraged to participate as much as possible in all activities alongside their peers and that you intervene only if necessary and after speaking to the pupil.

brilliant dos and don'ts

Do

✔ Develop a good (but professional!) relationship with the pupil by getting to know them and their parents.

✔ Ask your SENCO if you can read any paperwork relating to the pupil and for a copy of their IEP or BSP if you have not been involved in writing it.

✔ Always keep an eye out for any resources which may be useful.

Don't

✘ Have stereotypical views of pupils or their families.

✘ Try to take over or do work for pupils.

✘ Become personally involved with pupils and their families.

Working with parents

The Code of Practice was introduced in 2001 to make the process of identifying, assessing and supporting pupils with special educational needs more straightforward, and to give them an increased right to education in a mainstream school. It also increased the level of support available to parents and families of these pupils and involved them more in the process, so that it became more of a partnership. As a result, if you are working with a pupil who has special educational needs, you should find that you are working closely both with pupils and families as part of your role.

The most important area to remember when working with parents is that lines of communication will need to be kept open at all times. You will need to establish a positive relationship with them in order to ensure that the flow of information between home and school is continuous. The relationship should be one of mutual

> lines of communication will need to be kept open at all times

support and co-operation as both the school and parents will have the pupil's interests at the heart of all they do.

The school will need to make sure that parents have regular information about the pupil's progress, are aware of any intervention which is made, and are encouraged to contribute in any way which may support their child. They will need to consult parents before referring the pupil to any other professional. The school should also ensure that they are as supportive as possible to parents, who may be under pressure due to their child's needs, and respect their contributions and points of view. All schools should have a member of staff who is a family support worker, and, if you are supporting an individual pupil, you may need to work alongside this staff member.

Parents should be asked to support the school by giving them information as they will have the most expertise on their child and their needs. They will need to feel welcome in school and able to raise any concerns that they have about the pupil.

Working with outside agencies

There are a number of different agencies with whom you may come into contact when working with pupils who have special educational needs. These will mainly be based outside school and pupils will usually have appointments during or after lessons. However, they may also act in an advisory role and come to the school to give support for strategies which may be used when working with pupils who have special educational needs. If you are starting to work with an individual pupil, you will need to find out those agencies who are working with the pupil and whether you need to be present at any meetings which take place. The main agencies with whom you may come into contact are described below.

Speech and language therapist (SLT)

The speech and language therapist will give support to pupils with a range of difficulties. These may be issues such as problems with articulation or minor speech impairment to more complex language disorders. The pupil will need to be referred to the speech therapist either through their GP or the school, and will usually be given six-week 'blocks' of therapy as well as work for pupils and families to do at home as well as advice for the school. The SENCO will also liaise with the SLT to continue work in school on a day-to-day basis until the next block of therapy.

Occupational therapist (OT)

The occupational therapist will work with pupils on programmes to develop their fine motor skills. These are to do with the level of control they have over their hands (for example, cutting, threading, fastenings, and pen and pencil control). They will develop individual programmes for pupils to use at home, as well as giving advice for activities that they can work on at school.

Physiotherapist

The physiotherapist will work with pupils on programmes to develop their gross motor skills. These are to do with the level of control they have over their arms and legs (for example, walking, running, jumping, waving, throwing and so on). They will develop individual programmes for pupils to use at home, as well as giving advice for activities that they can work on at school.

Educational psychologist (EP)

The educational psychologist will come in and work with the school to assess pupils who are a cause for concern and to decide whether it is appropriate for them to go for a statutory assessment. They will usually come into school once a term. Often the educational psychologist will work long term with specific pupils if the school has concerns and will meet with parents and staff to devise learning plans and will write reports.

Sensory support teacher

When a school starts working with a pupil who has sensory support needs, the sensory support teacher will come into school to advise staff how to prepare the learning environment and give advice about managing their needs. For example, the school may need advice and/or equipment if they have a pupil with a hearing or visual impairment.

Autism advisory teacher

This teacher will be a specialist in working with pupils who have autistic spectrum disorder and will regularly come in to school to observe and devise specific strategies for individuals. If you are working with an autistic pupil it is likely that you will have some contact with this teacher.

brilliant tip

Make sure you know about any external professionals who work with individual pupils you support. If they write reports or advice for the school, your SENCO should give you a copy.

Working with your SENCO and understanding their role

If you are working with pupils who have special educational needs it is likely that you will be managed by or have a close relationship with your SENCO (Special Educational Needs Co-ordinator). The SENCO is responsible for the day-to-day co-ordination of educational provision for pupils in the school with special educational needs. They will usually be a member of the school's senior management team, although this is not always the case. It is likely that they will have a large workload as they will be responsible for managing the paperwork not only for pupils with statements but also all intervention programmes in the school and all pupils who have IEPs or BSPs. As well as advising other school staff, they will also need to co-ordinate the advice and reports written by external professionals, as well as managing appointments between these professionals and parents and teaching staff.

The role of the SENCO has in the past sometimes been taken by non-qualified teachers and has in some schools become a non-teaching post due to the workload, but this will depend on the school and the number of pupils. It is intended that from September 2011, all SENCOs will be qualified teachers, and there is now a national qualification available for SENCOs new to the role.

You should have time set aside with the SENCO to discuss any issues which come up in your work with pupils. This may mean going through new reports or strategies which have been suggested, so that you can work out how to fit these in to the pupils' timetable, and also to discuss any issues both before and after any meetings with parents and external agencies. The school should also have a SENCO assistant, who should have

> have time set aside with the SENCO

some time set aside to give support with administration. It is important that the assistant and SENCO also have some time together each week to discuss issues and catch up.

brilliant case study

You are working as an individual support assistant for Bhumika, who is in Year 5. She is autistic and consequently also has problems with speech and language. The autism advisory teacher comes into school once a term to observe Bhumika and to speak to you, and then separately to Bhumika's parents and the SENCO. He writes a report which gives suggested targets for Bhumika's IEP, which he goes through with you and always tells you that you will have a copy.

However, in the eighteen months you have been at the school you have never received a copy. You have asked the SENCO several times and, although she always says that she will pass it on to you, this has not happened. You can only assume that this is because she is always so busy.

● Why is it important that you should get to see the report?

● What would you do in this situation?

Working in a special school

Special schools exist as provision for pupils whose needs cannot be met in a mainstream school. They may specialise in specific conditions or needs, such as pupil behaviour, or may be for pupils who have moderate, severe or profound learning difficulties. If you are working in a special school, it is likely that your role will vary from day to day, depending on the needs of the children. In some special schools, all support staff will support all pupils, as there will be fewer numbers and all staff will know all pupils, whilst in others you may support a named pupil. You may be given a different timetable depending on the day and who is available, or you may have the same routine. You may also need to have additional training depending on the school and the needs of the pupils; for example, if you are required to carry out lifting or are asked to work on specific physio or occupational therapy with pupils, or need training in the use of equipment.

Depending on the school, you may not have as much contact with parents as at a mainstream school, as in some special schools the pupils will arrive and leave each day in special transport buses. However, parents will be encouraged to participate in the life of the school in other ways.

brilliant recap

- Make sure you know all you can about the needs of the pupil you support.
- Work with parents and involve them in their child's progress.
- Be sensitive to the needs of pupils and their families.
- Make sure you go for any training that is available on the pupil's needs or condition.
- Be aware of any external professionals who may work with the pupil.
- Work closely with your SENCO.

Further reading

- Dix, Paul (2009) *Taking Care of Behaviour*, Pearson.
- www.nasen.org.uk – National Association for Special Educational Needs.

CHAPTER 6

Working with pupils who speak English as an additional language

According to government statistics, English is now spoken as a second language by one in eight pupils in British schools. Many teaching assistants support these pupils either as an English speaker or as a bilingual assistant – that is, speaking to pupils in their native language in order to help them to access the curriculum. If you support bilingual or multilingual pupils, you will need to have an awareness of how all children process language and the importance for bilingual pupils of retaining their identity through valuing their home culture and language. You should also think about how aspects of culture, religion, home and family circumstances and upbringing can affect pupil learning. This chapter will also identify strategies for promoting pupils' language development in speaking and listening, reading and writing in English. Bilingual assistants may also be employed to provide support for pupils and families and to assess their abilities in their home language.

The process of language development

So that we can build a picture of how we learn language, it is important to think about the two stages which linguists consider that all children pass through. These are known as the pre-linguistic and the linguistic stages.

The pre-linguistic stage is during the first 12 months, when babies begin to learn the skills of basic communication. During this time, they will start to attract the attention of adults and repeat back the different sounds that they hear. This is true of any language, but although babies worldwide are born with the potential to make the same sounds, by the age of 12 months they can only repeat back the sounds that they have heard around them during that time.

The linguistic stage is when babies start to use the words that they hear and learn how to put sentences together. Children will develop this stage gradually over the next few years so that by the age of about five years they are fluent in their home language. For children who are learning more than one language from the earliest stages, however, learning to speak may be slightly slower as they will need to absorb different language systems.

Table 6.1 shows the stages of language development in children who speak one language. Adults will need to support them through

Table 6.1 Stages of language development

Age	Stage of development
0–6 months	Babies try to communicate through crying, starting to smile and babbling. They start to establish eye contact with adults.
6–18 months	Babies start to speak their first words. They start to use gestures to indicate what they mean. At this stage, they are able to recognise and respond to pictures of familiar objects.
18 months to 3 years	Children start to develop their vocabulary rapidly and make up their own sentences. At this stage, children enjoy simple and repetitive rhymes and stories.
3–8 years	Children start to use more and more vocabulary and the structure of their language becomes more complex. As they develop their language skills, they are able to use language in a variety of situations.
8+ years	Children continue to develop the complexity of their language skills and their confidence in the use of language should begin to flourish.

all of these stages in order to encourage and promote language development. Although you will be working with school age children, you should remember that bilingual or multilingual pupils may be at an earlier stage of development with their language.

If children have learned two or more languages simultaneously from an early age and they have been able to listen to good language models, it is likely that they will be confident in them and be able to 'switch' languages. When learning two languages together, children will need to be able to tune in to the language with the person who is speaking to them – in this way it will be easier for them to distinguish between the different languages. Problems may arise, however, if one parent, for example, regularly switches languages, as the child will find it difficult to know which language they are listening to at any given time. Once languages are established and the child grows older and more confident, this will be less important.

As an adult working in an educational setting, the most important thing for you to be aware of is the importance of language development as a route to learning. Language is the basis for

> we need to support all children to develop language skills

the way in which we organise our thoughts, ideas and feelings. We need to support all children to develop language skills and to build on their knowledge so that they are more able to access the curriculum.

brilliant tip

You should be aware that, when learning a new language, it is normal to have a 'silent phase' when the learner is 'tuning in' to new sounds and vocabulary. Try not to push learners into speaking English until they are ready.

Finding out about the pupil's background

If you are working with bilingual pupils who are new to your school you will need to find out as much as you can about their home and educational background and circumstances so that you can support them more effectively. Schools may do this in different ways:

- **Background forms:** The school will have a system for gathering initial information from parents or carers through forms. These will usually request basic information, medical details, child's position in the family, previous schools and languages spoken.

- **Home visits:** Depending on your school and the age of the pupil, a home visit may be carried out to find out more about the pupil and their home background. These may be varied – for example, pupils may have been brought up in the UK, have had a traumatic background or be asylum seekers. Alternatively, if parents do not speak any English the school may decide to invite them to school with an interpreter so that they can speak to them more directly.

- **Records from previous schools:** If the pupil has been to school in the UK before, their previous school will be asked to send transfer records and information about their progress, including their ability in the target language. They may also contain records from other agencies if these have been involved in working with the pupil, such as speech therapists (for more on other agencies see Chapter 5 page 85). However, be aware that these forms can sometimes take some time to arrive and may not be at your school before the pupil starts. Your SENCO or teachers may need to call the previous school and speak to staff there if necessary in order to gather information.

Once you have gathered initial information on the pupil you will have a clearer idea about their needs and be able to work with teachers to devise how they should be assessed and their needs met.

The importance of valuing cultural diversity

Depending on the pupil's home background and experiences, they may find starting at school very difficult, particularly if they have not been in an educational environment before. They may be having or have had to make significant adjustments: although some bilingual and multilingual pupils learn to speak their languages simultaneously from an early age, not all will be doing this and some may have only just started to learn a second or third language when you meet them. Pupils may feel isolated in this case, particularly if their language or culture is not the same as the majority of pupils in the school, and it is important for them to feel that the school values cultural diversity. Knowing that their culture and status is valued helps them to feel settled and secure, factors which will contribute to their being able to develop skills in a new language. Moreover, children need to want to learn; if they are feeling isolated or anxious, it is more likely that this will be difficult for them.

> children need to want
> to learn

The school should also encourage the involvement of all parents in the life of the school as much as possible; this is important both to encourage communication and to ensure that the pupil feels that the school and family value one another (see also pages 84–5 regarding communication with families). There will be measures in place in the school's equality policy to ensure that the whole school community recognises and celebrates a variety of religious and cultural festivals through assemblies, displays and trips, and encourages pupils to find out about other languages and faiths through religious and Personal, Social and Health Education (PSHE).

Find a copy of your school's equality and diversity policy. What kinds of examples can you find of the ways in which the school values and promotes cultural diversity?

The role of self-esteem in developing communication

It is helpful if all staff are made aware if a pupil who is new to the school does not speak English. This is because, as well as feeling that they fit in, pupils' self-esteem and confidence will be affected by their perception of how others see them. It is especially important for everyone to know and pronounce their name correctly. If their parents do not speak English, this may be a pupil's first experience of having to communicate with others in a language other than their own. It is important for the pupil to be able to communicate in school, and although they will usually pick up a new language reasonably quickly, this can be a difficult time for them and you should be sensitive to this. If you notice that a pupil is having problems it is important to discuss this with teachers as there will be strategies that you can put in place to support them.

Spend time with the pupil at breaktimes and encourage them to socialise with others through playground games, or give them a buddy or assign someone that they can go to if they need to find something out or are unsure of what to do.

🡕 brilliant case study

Sobiga is a new pupil in your class who does not speak any English. Although she has made friends and is involved in class activities, you have noticed that at breaktimes and lunchtimes she is often on her own.

- What kind of support does Sobiga need and why?
- List some strategies that you could use to help her to develop her self-esteem and language skills.

How to support the language skills of bilingual and multilingual pupils

Although pupil learning in general may be affected by their background and you will need to know about this and be sensitive to it (see also Chapter 3, pages 42–6 for factors affecting learning), your focus when working with bilingual pupils will be on the development of their language. You may be working with individuals or groups of pupils to help them with their speaking and listening, reading

> your focus will be on the development of their language

or writing. Although the approach you take with very young children may be different from that which you use with older pupils, the strategies you use should be similar and should apply across the curriculum.

Your initial work with pupils should be based on an assessment of their level of language as well as their level of ability. You should have guidance and support either from your SENCO or from teachers, and this will be the starting point for any individual work or targets which are devised for the pupil, who may be at different stages in their development of English. Remember that a pupil's ability to speak another language does not necessarily mean that they have a special educational need. The SENCO may be involved in devising educational plans for pupils who are at the earliest stages of learning English as an additional language; it is important that their progress is monitored and that they settle into school. However, although at the initial stages of learning a language these pupils may need extra support, learning a second language is not an indicator of either higher or lower ability.

Speaking and listening skills

As in all learning situations, the effective use of praise is very important when working with pupils who speak English as an additional language. You need to provide encouragement and support to these pupils as they will be insecure about the way in which they use their second language. Other strategies you will need to use will include the following.

Making opportunities to talk

Bilingual pupils will need to be given as much opportunity as possible to talk and discuss ideas with others. At a very young age this would include opportunities such as role play, whereas older pupils may enjoy debates and discussions around a set topic. Sometimes having a talk partner will help if pupils are less confident before putting their ideas forward in a larger group – the talk partner could be you or one of their peers. Remember that older pupils may be more self-conscious about speaking another language than younger ones.

Purposeful listening

You will need to make sure that you give pupils your full attention when speaking and listening with them. If you actively listen and respond to what they are saying, you will encourage them to do the same. In addition you will need to support pupils in class by repeating and checking pupil understanding of what the teacher has said. You should also ensure that you give pupils thinking time without rushing them, so that they are able to formulate a response to any questions.

When giving pupils feedback in learning situations and repeating back words or phrases to them, you may need to 'remodel' language or extend their responses through questioning. For example, if they use language incorrectly, such as 'I go to the shops at the weekend', you could respond 'You went to the shops last weekend? What did you buy?' rather than specifically pointing out an error.

Specific vocabulary

If pupils have come into school with very limited experience of the target language, you may be asked to work with them on specific areas of language – for example, the teacher may be focusing on positional words to ensure that pupils understand vocabulary such as behind, above, below, next to and so on. You may need to work with pictures or other resources to help pupils to develop their understanding of these words.

Songs and rhymes

Young children develop concepts of pattern and rhyme in language through learning nursery rhymes and songs. These are also an enjoyable way of developing language skills as well as being part of a group. If you are a bilingual assistant, you may also be able to introduce rhymes and songs in other languages for all the pupils to learn and so extend their cultural awareness.

Games

These are useful for developing language as they encourage pupils to interact with others at the same time as practising their language skills.

Physical cues and gestures

Physical cues and gestures such as thumbs up and down, raised eyebrows, and other forms of non-verbal communication will enable pupils to make sense of a situation more quickly, as well as act as a form of encouragement.

brilliant dos and don'ts

Do

✔ Involve bilingual pupils in purposeful talk as much as possible.

✔ Allow pupils more thinking time to prepare for what they want to say.

✔ Model correct use of language for them rather than correcting them.

✔ Give visual examples where possible.

Don't

✗ Answer questions for bilingual pupils.

✗ Put pupils who speak additional languages in groups with lower ability pupils, or group them all together.

✗ Ask pupils to 'say something' in their language to demonstrate to others unless there is a purpose to their doing it.

You will also need to remember that there is a difference between the social language in which pupils may be starting to become fluent at the earlier stages, and 'classroom' language. This is because in social situations the meaning of what is being communicated is often backed up by visual cues. It may also be different to the correct form of written English. Classroom language is likely to be more abstract, particularly in the case of older pupils, and it can be hard for them to tune into the kinds of functional language required in some learning situations, for example, hypothesising, evaluating, predicting and inferring. It is likely that there will be less visual demonstration to support learning – you will need to

> classroom language is likely to be more abstract

be able to give practical support to pupils and continue to check their understanding of what is being asked.

Reading and writing skills

As you are developing the speaking and listening skills of bilingual pupils, you will also need to be able to find opportunities to support their reading and writing skills in English. Pupils will need to be able to link the development of the spoken word with reading and writing and should participate in all lessons with their peers so that they can observe good practice from other pupils. However, if they need additional focused support, you may need to adapt or modify learning resources that others are using in order to help them to access the curriculum more fully. You may also need to explain and reinforce specific vocabulary if it is part of a topic or subject area. As with all other pupils, they will need to be able to experience a variety of texts, both fiction and non-fiction, in order to maximise their vocabulary.

brilliant activity

Find out about the different kinds of resources that are available in your school for supporting bilingual pupils. Were they easy to find? What was the source?

Liaising with support teachers

If you are working with bilingual or multilingual pupils, it is likely that you will also be asked to liaise with other support teachers. Usually there will be an external teacher who comes into school to support the SENCO and teachers to do more focused work regularly with bilingual pupils and to give advice. Assistants may be called upon to carry out initial assessments and also to follow up this work when needed, particularly when the support teacher has finished their allocated time in school.

Working as a bilingual assistant

If you are bilingual yourself, you may have been employed or asked by the school to use pupils' first language to support teaching and learning. You may also be involved in providing support for families and liaising with them in order to promote pupil participation. This role will often be created in schools which have a high percentage of bilingual learners to make it easier for the school to encourage communication between the school and families who do not speak English. If this is your role, you should have some opportunity to work with the governor or named teacher in the school who is responsible for advising teachers about EAL learners. You should also be able to feed back to teachers, in particular if there are concerns about specific pupils.

Communicating with families

As a bilingual assistant, it is likely that you will be involved in providing support and information to families. Parents of bilingual pupils may speak very little or no English themselves and in this situation the school will need to devise additional strategies to encourage their involvement and understanding. It is important that parents and carers feel able to approach the school and share information in order to maximise the opportunities to communicate.

be careful not to include your own opinions or ideas

However, you should remember that if you are passing information between school and families; that is all you should be doing. Be careful not to include your own opinions or ideas about what should be happening on either side without consulting with other staff first.

You may be communicating with parents and families from a range of backgrounds and some of these families may be facing difficult circumstances or need additional support which you are not able to provide. In this case, you should go through your SENCO or teacher responsible for EAL pupils to seek outside support from your local authority or social services to ensure that the school is offering as much help or advice as possible, and as a bilingual speaker you will be able to explain what support is available to families.

Working with pupils

Bilingual assistants will often support pupils who have a limited knowledge of English by assessing their ability in their home language. It is helpful to be able to gauge their level of fluency – if this is good it will be easier for them to learn a second language more quickly as they will have another language to relate it to. If you are working in a school with a high percentage of pupils who speak a particular language, you may support individuals or groups of pupils in order to help them to develop their English skills whilst also speaking to them in their first language. It can also help to detect any language disorder or learning delay which pupils may have, as these can take longer to become evident in pupils who speak additional languages. In this situation you will need to refer to your SENCO or to teachers who will need to refer the pupil for specialist assessment.

Giving feedback to pupils, families and colleagues

As a bilingual assistant it is likely that you will be involved in meetings and discussions with teachers and families about pupil progress. Pupils should also be fully involved in the procedure if possible. The best way in which to do this is to set aside a regular time with pupils and teachers to discuss their progress and to think about any additional support they might need. You may also be invited to parents' evenings and other events in order to support teachers and other staff in passing information on to parents. If you have been asked to do this, you should make time to speak to teachers beforehand so that you know what information the teachers need to have passed on and how they would like you to structure what you say.

You will also need to be able to give feedback to colleagues, particularly if the pupil speaks very little English. Colleagues will need you to pass on information about pupil development in English and also their knowledge and use of their home language, which may reflect their confidence in using language generally. For example, a pupil who has a working knowledge of one language already understands the purpose and process of how it works, and is more likely to be able to apply this to another language. The feedback you give to colleagues may be written or verbal depending on the school's policy, but it is best to keep a record of some kind so that the information is available to others if required at a later date.

---

keep a record of some kind

---

brilliant recap

- Find out as much as you can about the pupil from the earliest stages.
- Develop a good relationship with bilingual pupils and their families to encourage home–school communication.
- Encourage and value the contribution of all languages and cultures in school.
- Make sure you give positive feedback to pupils when working with them as much as you can.
- Keep an eye out for resources which may be useful.

Further reading

- www.britishcouncil.org – there is plenty of information here to support the development of relationships with partner schools in other countries.

- www.dfes.gov.uk – the Standards Site has information under EAL learners.

- www.freenglish.com – has resources for those wishing to learn English.

- www.mantrapublishing.com – this company produces a range of books in different languages.

- www.naldic.org.uk – the National Association for Language Development in the Curriculum aims to raise attainment of EAL learners; the website contains a number of links and resources.

- www.teachernet.gov.uk – type in 'EAL' under 'search'.

- www.qcda.gov.uk – A Language in Common, Assessing English as an additional language, 2000. This is a useful document to help with the assessment of bilingual pupils.

CHAPTER 7

Working with Gifted and Talented pupils

As part of your role as a teaching assistant, you may be asked to work with Gifted and Talented (G&T) pupils, whether this is through the support you give to individuals within the class or through work with groups from different year groups. You will need to work with others to develop learning programmes for these pupils to increase their opportunities and ensure that they are challenged within the class through strategies such as Assessment for Learning (AfL). Professionals both within and outside the school will be able to help with the identification and support you provide for these pupils.

What is a Gifted and Talented pupil?

In 2006, the then DFES defined Gifted and Talented pupils as 'Children and young people with one or more abilities developed to a level significantly ahead of their year group (or with the potential to develop these abilities).' According to the Standards Site (www.standards.dfes.gov.uk), the term has been further refined:

- **Gifted:** pupils who have or show the potential for exceptional academic abilities.
- **Talented:** pupils who have exceptional abilities or potential in art and design, PE or sports, music or performing arts such as dance and drama.

Gifted and Talented pupils will be those who are showing or have the potential for exceptional ability in the areas described above. An OFSTED report 'Providing for Gifted and Talented Pupils,' which evaluated provision for Gifted and Talented pupils in 2001, said at the time that many of these pupils had not been adequately challenged as part of curriculum provision in schools and was examining the progress which had been made in providing for them. Since then, progress has continued to be made in the support and provision which is available, including the introduction of the Gifted and Talented programme and the 2005 White Paper, 'Better Schools for All', which also stated that all pupils should be given opportunities to reach their potential. It aims to reach the top five to ten per cent of pupils in schools and to encourage the development of their skills and talents.

If you have been asked to work with Gifted and Talented pupils, you may have a particular talent yourself: you might, for example, be a talented artist, sportsperson or musician who is able to work with pupils to nurture their talent. Your role when supporting such pupils will be to work alongside teachers to use strategies which will enable pupils to develop the skills or talents they have. You may carry out work with pupils alongside others in class; alternatively you may work with small groups from different classes or year groups outside the class. In both of these situations, you should be given support and activities to carry out with pupils and should not have to devise these yourself. You may also have the input of the school's Gifted and Talented co-ordinator who will be able to give you additional support and strategies.

> enable pupils to develop the skills or talents they have

↗ brilliant case study

Richard is working in a secondary school as an assistant in the Music department. Although the current Year 7 have not been in school for long, he has noticed that one pupil in particular, Ahsan, seems to be showing a strong talent in both piano and cello. Ahsan does not have lessons at the school but has joined the lower school orchestra and is very keen on using the piano in the music room to practice for one of his grades the following week.

● What would you do if you were Richard?
● How could you ensure that Ahsan's talent is encouraged in school?

Recognising Gifted and Talented pupils

You may sometimes feel that you are working with pupils who are Gifted and Talented but that this has not yet been recognised by the school. This is possible because it may not always be apparent from the earliest stages. The characteristics in Figure 7.1 may be some of the indicators which you could look out for, although even one or two of these may mean that a pupil is particularly able.

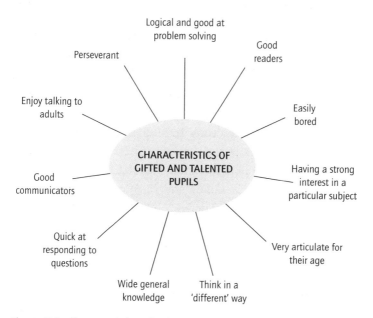

Figure 7.1 Characteristics of Gifted and Talented pupils

Pupils who may be Gifted and Talented will show some of these characteristics and you will need to discuss your observations with teachers as well as your school's Gifted and Talented Co-ordinator. You will then need to work with them to devise a plan for these pupils. Your school's equal opportunities or inclusion policy will give details of the school's expectations when supporting these pupils, or you may have a Gifted and Talented policy. Equal opportunities are the right of every child and it is important that schools make effective provision for those pupils who have particular talents and abilities. If you think that a pupil with whom you are working may be Gifted or Talented, observe them over time and write down some of the examples which you have noticed, then either speak to the school's co-ordinator or to the pupil's teacher.

↗ brilliant case study

Nadia is in Year 2 and is a very quiet pupil. Although you have known her for some time, you have noticed that she is becoming more confident and has started to be very quick at responding to the teacher in a range of situations. You start to observe her more carefully and within one week you are able to give several examples of situations in which she has shown a higher level of understanding than her peers.

- Should you automatically assume that Nadia is a Gifted and Talented pupil?
- What should you do next?

Motivating and challenging Gifted and Talented pupils

Once a pupil has been recognised as being Gifted or Talented, you may be asked to work with them on a regular basis following advice and guidelines from teachers. You should have a working knowledge of the current curriculum within which the pupil or pupils is working as well as knowing how it develops, so that along with teachers you can extend their learning. However, Gifted and Talented pupils should also be challenged by enriching and broadening their learning experience in as many ways as possible before taking them to the next level. Your school may have a Gifted and Talented register of pupils which should be updated regularly.

You will need to be very clear on your role so that you know how much and how often support should be in place, and whether you are working on specific targets that will be monitored. You should clarify, either through teachers or through the G & T co-ordinator, how your work with pupils will meet their needs most effectively. You should also know how often you can speak to others in order to check on pupil progress and to seek additional help if needed. If you are an experienced practitioner and know the pupil, you will be able to put forward your own suggestions about the planned activities and how these

be very clear on your role

may best be carried out. If you are involved with planning yourself with teachers you may be able to make suggestions about how you can use your own knowledge at the planning stage and how pupils may benefit. Your school may also seek advice from outside professionals. If a pupil has a particular talent in art, sport or music and does not have any outside encouragement, it is important that the school both investigates and suggests to parents how this may be accessed. It is particularly important that pupils from disadvantaged backgrounds are given additional support to encourage them to participate in activities outside school. Some schools may have extended provision outside school hours which gives pupils opportunities to develop their particular skills, whilst others might have access through local cluster groups. Increasingly, schools may work with local authorities to develop summer schools and you may be involved with the development and provision of either of these, although they may tend to be with older pupils. Your co-ordinator should also be able to help and advise you about the kinds of resources and equipment which may be available.

The main strategies which you should use with Gifted and Talented pupils should enable them to extend their thinking whilst working on the same kinds of activities which are being carried out by other pupils. They should also be able to work on open-ended tasks, which will give them opportunities to:

- **Work in more depth:** Pupils with whom you work should have learning experiences which encourage them to think in depth and question why things happen; for example 'Why do you think that the Romans needed to build aqueducts?'

- **Work in a broader range of contexts:** Pupils should be encouraged to apply what they have learned to different contexts; for example, if they are learning about materials and their properties they should consider what would happen if different materials were used to make everyday objects.

- **Work at their own pace:** As Gifted and Talented pupils will often have a greater understanding of new concepts and ideas than their peers, they should be able to work in an environment where they can achieve at their own pace without standing out from others. In order to be able to extend pupil thinking, you should also think about *how* you work with pupils and the expectations you have, as well as the way in which you approach learning.

- **Have high expectations:** It is important that within the school there is a climate of high expectation, not just for pupils who are Gifted and Talented but for everyone. Staff should encourage and challenge all pupils to develop their thinking skills as much as possible so that they are able to achieve to the best of their ability. Research has shown that where children are encouraged and told that they will be able to achieve, they are more likely to do so. This is known as the Pygmalion effect – if a person thinks that we are clever, they treat us this way, and we learn to think that we are. Positive expectations will lead to a more positive attitude to learning in the same way that negative self-expectation also leads to negative behaviour.

● **Act as a co-learner rather than a teacher:** Sometimes when working with pupils who are very able you may feel that they are more knowledgeable than you. This should not be a problem and pupils should not always be made to feel that adults know everything! Your role in this situation is to tell the pupil that you are going to find out together and use questions to support their thinking. It is more appropriate to use language such as 'What are we trying to find out?' or 'What can we do to help us?' rather than using the term 'you', as the learning is then seen as a shared experience. Pupils will also benefit from the feeling of learning as being seen as a process of discovery, rather than something that adults know already and that they have to find out.

● **Use challenging questioning to deepen thinking:** The way in which you question pupils will make a difference to the way in which they approach tasks. After speaking with teachers, you may like to use the different levels of thinking explored in Bloom's Taxonomy (see Figure 7.2 overleaf) as a starting point, as this is a good way of thinking about how questioning can do this. Benjamin Bloom, an educational psychologist working in the 1950s, devised this classification for measuring depth of learning. Since this was published, subsequent educational thinking has put the three higher levels of the pyramid as parallel, while some have swapped synthesis and evaluation over.

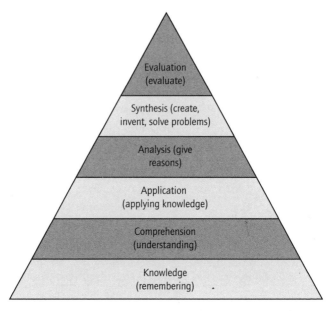

Figure 7.2 Bloom's taxonomy

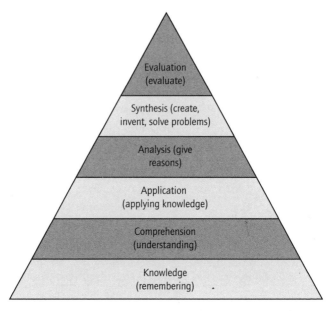 **brilliant** example

An example of how Bloom's Taxonomy works can be seen in the kinds of questions which can be asked at each level of questioning:

1   Knowledge – how many different kinds of potato can you name?

2   Comprehension – how and where do potatoes grow? What do you know about the process?

3   Application – which type of potato would you use for making the best mashed potato and why?

4   Analysis – list different examples of foods which are made from potatoes in order from most to least health benefits.

5   Synthesis – create your own recipe using potatoes.

6   Evaluation – what do you think about the way in which potatoes are used in different parts of the world? Explain your reasoning.

---

brilliant activity

See whether you can create your own questions using a current theme or topic you are working on in school using the different levels in Bloom's Taxonomy. How might this influence the way in which you question pupils?

brilliant tip

Gifted and Talented children may struggle with the concept of 'getting it wrong' sometimes. They may be so used to achieving that when tasks are more challenging or they are having difficulty, they become frustrated. This is another reason for setting them appropriate challenges. It is very important that these pupils understand the importance of learning through making mistakes and finding out that they might not always be able to work out the solution to a problem straight away.

Using Assessment for Learning

Pupils who are academically gifted should be given plenty of opportunities to think about how they can apply what they know in different situations and what it means to be active learners. Assessment for Learning is a way in which pupils are asked to take more responsibility for their own learning. Through it, pupils are able to understand the aim of what they are doing, what they need to do to reach that aim and where they are in relation to it through measuring their own progress. You may be asked to support them in doing this by clarifying pupils' understanding of learning objectives

> pupils are able to understand the aim of what they are doing

and making sure that they are on track with their learning. They can also be encouraged to peer-assess and to build up their techniques through working with adults and their peers so that they will be able to look more objectively at their own achievements. Assessment for Learning also supports the encouragement of high expectation by emphasising the achievement of pupils rather than focusing on what they can't do. Many schools are adopting Assessment for Learning for use in all age groups so that pupils can develop self-assessment skills and can reflect on and recognise their own achievements. Although it is used with all pupils, Gifted and Talented pupils can be encouraged to develop these skills further so that they can take on more responsibility for their own learning, become more active learners and support others.

When supporting Assessment for Learning, you will need to use different techniques and be aware of how they can enhance what pupils are doing, as well as knowing when you should refer to others (see Figure 7.3).

At the start of any activity, pupils need to be clear about what they are going to learn and how they will be assessed. For Assessment for Learning to be effective, pupils need to know what they are learning, why they are learning it and how the assessment will take place. If you are able to work on this with pupils they should be able to think about their learning after each activity and consider how their learning in the future may be affected.

brilliant activity

The next time you are working with a group of pupils, clarify the learning objectives and assessment criteria with pupils and encourage them to continue to check their learning against these throughout the session, either alone or with a partner. Consider how much careful management of pupil learning encourages them to achieve at a higher level.

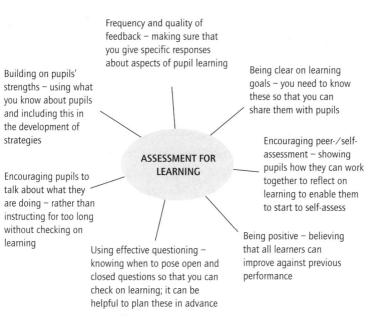

Figure 7.3 Strategies for supporting Assessment for Learning

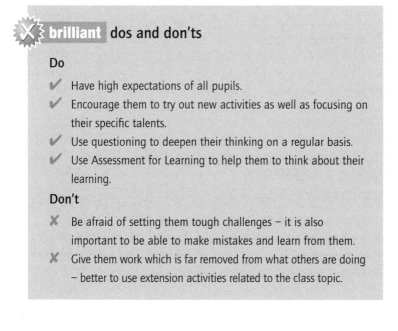

brilliant dos and don'ts

Do

✔ Have high expectations of all pupils.

✔ Encourage them to try out new activities as well as focusing on their specific talents.

✔ Use questioning to deepen their thinking on a regular basis.

✔ Use Assessment for Learning to help them to think about their learning.

Don't

✘ Be afraid of setting them tough challenges – it is also important to be able to make mistakes and learn from them.

✘ Give them work which is far removed from what others are doing – better to use extension activities related to the class topic.

brilliant recap

- Look out for Gifted and Talented pupils in all year groups.
- Make sure Gifted and Talented pupils are supported in different ways.
- Act as a co-learner and support pupils through the way in which you question their thinking.
- Use Assessment for Learning where you can.
- Encourage pupils to reflect on their learning strategies and achievements.
- Work with your G&T co-ordinator for support and advice.

Further reading

- www.Gifted-and-Talented.net
- www.nagc.org – National Association for Gifted Children.
- www.nagcbritain.org.uk – National Association of Gifted and Talented Youth.
- www.teachers.tv – this site has plenty of information, suggestions, links and videos to support a range of topics.

CHAPTER 8

Providing pastoral support

Part of your role as a teaching assistant will be to provide pastoral support to pupils. Generally speaking, pastoral support means any need a pupil may have which is not dealt with within the classroom. In other words, you are likely to be the adult whom pupils will approach with any issues or problems which they may feel that they are not able to talk about with others. Pupils may also confide in you to an extent where you may have to tell others due to particular concerns you may have. This work can sometimes be quite sensitive and you will need to be able to handle different situations appropriately whilst providing support to pupils. You may also be asked to support different stages in pupils' education by supporting teachers as they prepare pupils for different transitions, as well as working with pupils on citizenship and community projects. This chapter will also examine situations which arise on a regular basis, such as mentoring pupils, and also look at restorative justice which is becoming widely used in schools for resolving conflict situations.

Providing general support to pupils

As part of your role, you will be managing pupils' pastoral needs on a daily basis. These may range from disagreements during breaktimes to concerns about homework, worries due to issues at home, or friendship and social problems. As well as providing general guidance, this may sometimes involve talking about quite complex issues which are happening in pupils' lives either within or outside school, such as bullying, bereavement, family breakdown, drug and alcohol dependency, or children as carers. You may be approached in different situations and at different stages for advice, support and reassurance. Pupils may come to you simply because you are approachable, or because you work in this capacity, for example as a learning mentor or family worker, in which case you should have had some additional training – see examples below.

brilliant examples

In Charlotte's primary school, she runs a 'Listening ear' club which is open during morning break three times per week. The club is to encourage any pupils who need to talk to an adult to come and do this and to know that there is an adult there at set times who is able to listen. Charlotte has been able to talk to pupils who have worries and to support them in finding a way to work these through. She has been on additional training through the school and also holds a counselling qualification.

Shereen is a learning support assistant for Elysha in Year 7 who has sensory needs and regularly works with whole groups of pupils, as well as the girl she supports. She is required to be on duty during breaktimes and lunchtimes and as a result frequently has to deal with disagreements and disputes by talking them through with pupils.

It is likely that you will also provide regular pastoral support to pupils during the school day – teaching assistants are often in a position to do this as they may have more time and opportunity than teachers. This is an integral part of your role and you will need to reassure pupils that it is good to talk about their feelings and that you will help them as much as you can.

reassure pupils that it is good to talk about their feelings

You should be aware that, whilst pupils may come to you and seek advice and reassurance, you may need to consult with other staff as well as your school's child protection or safeguarding policy in order to ensure that you handle them correctly, especially if you suspect some kind of abuse (see Brilliant dos and don'ts below). If a pupil decides to confide in you, it is very important that you explain to them that you will need to tell another adult.

As well as listening to pupils who may confide in you, you should also be on the look out for signs of abuse. Remember that there are different kinds of abuse which can also be passive, i.e. the abuser has neglected in their duty of care for the child, either physically or emotionally. (For more on the signs of abuse and what to do, see Chapter 9 page 155.)

brilliant dos and don'ts

Do

✔ Tell them that they have done the right thing in talking to someone.

✔ Tell them that you believe them.

✔ Say that you will help them.

Don't

✗ Ask the pupil too many questions about what has happened.

✗ Make promises about what will or won't happen.

✗ Tell them that you won't tell anyone else.

After you have spoken with the pupil you will need to inform the designated member of staff for child protection – make sure you know who this person is in your school in case you need to speak to them urgently about a pupil. You should also make written notes of what the pupil has told you straight away so that you can pass on the details as soon as possible.

Supporting transition

Whatever age group you are working with, it is likely that at some stage you will be supporting them as they move classes. Whether this change is within the same school or to prepare them for moving on, either to another school or the outside world, transition can be traumatic for some pupils. You will need to work closely with teachers and develop strategies to support pupils as they pass through transitions at different stages.

Starting school

If you are working with the youngest age group in school, you will be involved in supporting pupils through one of the biggest changes they have experienced. The school will have a series of steps in place to ensure that children and families are supported through a time which can be challenging for both sides.

Usually when starting school, teachers will have visited either the child's home or nursery if it is not attached to the school, so that they can be introduced to the child. They may also have a series of introductory sessions during the term before the child starts school so that children can experience being in school and meet some of their peers and existing reception children, especially if they are starting school in January.

> spend plenty of time talking and getting to know pupils

If you are working with this age group, make sure you spend plenty of time talking and getting to know pupils during the first few weeks of school, as well as carrying out the necessary observations and so gaining a clear picture of each child, particularly if you are their key worker. (For more on the EYFS see Chapter 2 page 22.)

Reception to Year 1

The transition from reception to Year 1 should not be as much of a challenge to pupils as their initial entry into school, in particular since the Foundation Stage curriculum is now extended for the first term that the child is in Year 1 as part of the transition process. However, although this is the case, Year 1 can still be very different. Pupils may not have participated in whole school activities such as assemblies and breaktimes with older children, and there may be fewer adults in a Year 1 classroom when pupils have been used to having their own key worker. It is likely that at this time teachers in this year group will meet for a handover meeting to share information about each child and to discuss their Foundation Stage Profiles, and to highlight children with special educational needs. This will then occur at the same time of year in subsequent changes of form.

brilliant tip

Whatever year group you support, ask if you can be present at this handover meeting at the start of the school year so that you can find out about the needs of the pupils in advance. If possible, also speak to your SENCO about any pupils who have additional needs.

Year 2 to Year 3

Depending on the school or schools, the transfer from Year 2 to Year 3 may be no more of a challenge than any other year group. In many primary schools transferring to the juniors may simply be moving upstairs or to a different corridor. However, in some cases, pupils will be physically moving schools when transferring from Key Stage 1 to Key Stage 2. Even though these schools may be on the same site, they will frequently be housed in different buildings. In this situation or if pupils are changing sites, it is important for staff to manage the handover carefully and ensure that pupils have plenty of time both with their new teacher and have a chance to look around and speak to others in the school.

Year 6 to Year 7

This transition is usually managed carefully as pupils will be starting a completely new phase in their schooling. If you are working in a Year 6 class it is likely that during the summer term you will be carrying out projects and activities and having discussions around the subject of secondary school. These activities will encourage pupils to start to focus on secondary school and also to talk about their concerns and any anxieties which they may have. Year 6 teachers will liaise with the head of year from Year 7 where possible to discuss the needs of pupils and to address any concerns. Similarly, the start of Year 7 will need to be managed carefully so that pupils learn to be more responsible for organising themselves around issues such as timetabling and homework, which will be difficult to start with.

brilliant case study

Jean-Paul works in a small village primary school where the pupils usually transfer to a number of much larger secondary schools in the area. He spends his time as a teaching assistant in a mixed Year 5/6 class and is presently working with the teacher to manage the leavers' production and to ensure that the transition process goes smoothly.

- Why is it particularly important in Jean-Paul's school to manage transition actively and to reassure pupils about any concerns which they may have?
- How might Jean-Paul be involved in the process?

Leaving school

This can be a difficult transition to manage as pupils will usually leave school following their last exams. The process will need to be driven by teachers and support staff throughout the last year of school and in particular if pupils are intending to leave following GCSEs. You may be approached by pupils at this time if they are finding it difficult to decide which options to take and need some support in doing this. You may need to refer them to your school's careers teachers or for additional support outside school, such as the Connexions service which offers support and advice to 13–19-year-olds.

Mentoring

Learning mentors were originally introduced as part of the government's Excellence in Cities initiative in 2001. This was designed to improve inner-city education through a range of measures, which also included the Gifted and Talented programme. As part of the initiative, learning mentors were recruited to support schools in raising standards, improving attendance and reducing exclusions through working closely with individual pupils. The role of the learning mentor has become a key part of the role of some support staff, and some are employed with mentor as part of their job title. Learning mentors are involved in helping to remove barriers to learning and to raise pupil achievement in school with pupils of all ages. They will work alongside teachers to set targets and support pupils in developing their confidence and looking at ways of improving their work.

The kinds of skills an effective mentor will need are an extension of those required for the role of teaching assistant. Learning mentors need to be good listeners, develop good relationships with their mentees and offer support through talking through issues. They will also need to be able to encourage and

learning mentors need to be good listeners

motivate pupils, in particular in cases of low self-esteem and disaffection with school. However, in order to be a learning mentor you should also be sent on specific training to ensure that you are fully prepared for your role.

A learning mentor is a:

- role model

- active listener

- observer

- encourager

- professional friend

- challenger of assumptions

- guide

- target negotiator

- reliable, approachable, non-judgemental and realistic supporter – with pupils, parents and staff.

A learning mentor is not a:

- counsellor

- classroom assistant

- babysitter

- disciplinarian

- person to whom a pupil is sent when naughty.

Source: *Good Practice Guidelines for Learning Mentors* (DFES, 2001)

The mentoring process should be regulated through your local authority and it is likely that there will be a link learning mentor who will be able to establish local networks and share good practice between schools and local services, as well as directing schools to other local and national groups. Learning mentors should not work in isolation and your school should set up an initial mentoring action plan after discussing the pupil's needs with their family and involving other services where these are needed (see Figure 8.1). Your role will include working with pupils on all aspects of school life, whether this is to do with

Figure 8.1 Other services potentially involved

learning, socialising with others, managing their own needs or with anger management issues.

External services will work with the school to support and monitor the effectiveness of the mentoring process, in particular with regard to pupil progress and attendance. They may also provide resources and further training, as well as attending meetings between local mentoring cluster groups. If you are asked to be involved in mentoring, make sure that you find out as much as you can about both the pupil and the way in which the school manages the process. This may involve speaking to your school's SENCO or inclusion manager about the kinds of activities you are to undertake with particular pupils and the time allocated to do this.

Working on Citizenship activities with pupils

The subject of Citizenship is part of the curriculum, and along with Personal, Social and Health Education (PSHE) often takes place alongside and through other subjects, or through the wider work of the school. Through Citizenship activities, pupils are encouraged to learn about themselves and how to keep safe, as well as developing skills and rules for keeping healthy. This develops as they progress through school into learning about and understanding their own responsibilities for themselves and for the environment, and becoming more aware of their own responsibilities as part of their community and the wider world. They will be encouraged to develop social skills such as helping others, resolving their own arguments and resisting bullying, as well as making more informed choices about their own health and the environment.

> pupils are encouraged to learn about themselves and how to keep safe

In this way, Citizenship promotes the ideal that pupils will become responsible and active members of their own communities and have an understanding of the interdependence of these within the wider world.

As the term 'community cohesion' has become a focus in most schools, it is now likely that as part of the school, you may be involved in projects and issues within the local community. Schools and families are encouraged to be proactive in setting up and supporting local events, fundraising and other links so that pupils become more involved and active citizens. You may be asked to support or lead projects in which pupils are asked to work alongside others with these basic ideas in mind.

brilliant case study

Sally works as a teaching assistant in Year 5, whose topic at present is 'What is my carbon footprint?' She has been working with the class to try to think of ways to save energy and encourage others to do the same. As part of this project they have decided to write to the local council and ask them to review recycling in the borough's schools to include more materials as at the moment they just recycle paper.

● How will this idea support community cohesion as well as enhancing what the pupils are doing as part of the curriculum?

Schools will also usually have their own school council which will include representatives from each year group. These pupils will meet regularly, making decisions and speaking to the rest of the school about issues which concern the whole school community. A teacher will be involved with co-ordinating the school council but there may also be support staff involved. School councils should have a high profile in the school and other pupils should be able to nominate items to be discussed as well as vote on whole school issues.

brilliant activity

Find out about the kinds of activities or links your school has initiated or supported as part of community cohesion. How have pupils worked alongside others or developed links which have been beneficial locally?

Working with pupils on restorative justice

One of the most challenging aspects of school for some pupils is to learn how to understand and respect the feelings of others. Young children in particular find this difficult as their maturity and understanding are not developed enough for them to put themselves in the position of others. We often speak to them in school about how they should consider the consequences of their actions and how these may have affected others. Through stories, assemblies and role play and during circle time and

PSHE and Citizenship activities we might encourage them to think about others' feelings.

Restorative justice is a strategy which has been applied in schools following its successful implementation in the criminal justice system both at home and abroad. It has worked well as a method of resolving behaviour issues and learning from the consequences. Restorative justice is a helpful method of demonstrating to pupils what impact their behaviour will have on others through encouraging both parties to sit together and talk about what has happened. This method of conflict resolution has become a tried and tested means of supporting pupils through issues such as bullying and restoring positive relationships. It may take place through PSHE sessions, assemblies and role play, or through focused group sessions which develop pupils' ability to listen to others and respect their feelings. Restorative justice sessions can be run by any trained member of school staff and will be slightly different in primary and secondary schools, although they follow the same principles. They may be run with small or large groups, so may be just two people with a mediator, or a circle time session to deal with problem solving.

> encourage them to think about others' feelings

🡒 brilliant case study

Amal has been working in a secondary school for 4 months and is based in Years 7 and 8. He has been trained in restorative justice techniques at his previous school and also speaks Hindu. There have been some cases of racist bullying amongst the girls in the two year groups during breaktimes and Amal suggests to the head of Year 7 that he should run some sessions.

● What should Amal do first?

● What kind of form could the sessions take?

brilliant recap

- Make sure you always take the time to listen to pupils.
- Follow up on any issues which pupils have discussed with you.
- Be alert to any safeguarding or child protection issues.
- Work with teachers to ensure transition is managed effectively.
- Seek training if you are involved in additional strategies for supporting pastoral care such as mentoring or restorative justice.

Further reading

- www.nmn.org.uk – National Mentoring Network.
- www.cwdcouncil.org.uk – useful information about learning mentors.
- www.transformingconflict.org – for more on restorative justice.
- QCDA (2010) 'Community Cohesion in Action'.

CHAPTER 9

Health, safety, first aid and safeguarding

This chapter will examine the importance of being aware of health and safety issues in your school. All staff have a responsibility to maintain the learning environment and know the expectations of their role in different situations to show that they assist with the safety and protection of children and young people. This extends to knowing about the Health and Safety at Work Act, risk assessments, following school policy and using safety equipment. You should know how to respond to sickness, accidents and emergencies and how to record this as well as first aid requirements.

Following the tragic case of Victoria Climbié, the Children Act of 2004 has meant that there has been wide-ranging reform in the area of children's services and safeguarding. The Every Child Matters framework and increased safeguarding for children and young people highlights the need for all those working in schools to encourage pupils to keep themselves safe.

Health and safety in the learning environment

Schools need to ensure that they take measures to protect pupils and other adults at all times whilst they are on school premises, but also when accompanying pupils on school trips. This means that there will be health and safety procedures in place for a number of situations that may arise, including the following.

Accidents, emergencies and first aid

There should be enough first aiders in the school at any time
or when on school trips to deal with accidents and you should
be aware of who they are – schools will usually display their
names close to first aid boxes. First aid boxes should be regularly
checked and replenished.

School security and strangers

This includes making sure that all those who are in the school
have been accounted for through being identified and signed in.
Schools will have different ways of doing this; for example, visitors may be issued with badges. If you
notice any unidentified people in the
school, you should challenge them
immediately – this can simply be by
asking if you can help them in any
way. If you notice anything suspicious, you should always send for
help. Schools may also have secure entry and exit points, which
may make it more difficult for individuals to enter the premises.

> challenge unidentified
> people immediately

Fire and school evacuation procedures

Your school will have procedures in place so that everyone
knows what to do in case the building needs to be evacuated.
Fire drills should take place regularly (at least once a term) and
at different times of day. This is to ensure that pupils and all staff
are prepared, including midday supervisors and kitchen staff or
those responsible for extended school provision.

Personal hygiene

Pupils will from an early age develop routines and good practice
for general personal hygiene and understand its importance.
You should be a good role model for pupils, for example, talking
about the importance of washing your hands before carrying out
cooking activities, or after handling animals.

General health and safety

This should be a regular topic at staff meetings, during assemblies and as part of the general school culture so that everyone's attention is drawn to the fact that health and safety is a shared responsibility.

Controls on substances harmful to health (COSHH)

Anything which could be harmful should be stored out of pupils' reach or locked away in a cupboard – for example, cleaning materials or medicines. COSHH legislation gives a step-by-step list of precautions that need to be taken in order to prevent any risk or injury.

Things to look out for

As a general rule, you should be vigilant to health and safety issues in all situations but your routines should help to ensure that you keep the environment free from hazards. Remember also that, the younger the child, the less aware of risks they may be in the environment so you will need to modify your level of supervision according to their needs.

Ensure rooms are organised and laid out safely

This is common sense but furniture should be the correct size for pupils and well spaced out, and there should always be clear access to fire exits and internal doors. As part of your role as a member of support staff you should assist in keeping equipment organised and in the correct place and encourage pupils to do the same. Outdoor areas should also be checked prior to use; for example, if you are working in the Foundation Stage you will routinely need to check for any litter, broken glass or animal mess before children go outside, and sandpits will need to be covered when not in use to ensure that they are clean. If you are working in a specified area of the school grounds, you should also check this before going outside with pupils.

Check furniture, equipment and materials as a matter of course
The person responsible for health and safety in your setting should routinely carry out walkrounds on a regular basis to check that no hazards are left unreported. However, you should also check equipment before using it and if you notice anything broken or damaged, make sure that you remove and label it if possible so that pupils are not able to use it. You should then inform the person responsible – your school may have a book for doing this or you may be able to speak to them directly. All electrical items in school as well as fire equipment should also have annual checks by a qualified person and these should be recorded.

Adapt the environment to ensure safety for any pupils with SEN
All pupils within the class should be given equal opportunities and this should be remembered when setting out the environment. If you are working with a pupil who has special educational needs, you will know what considerations or adaptations need to be made for them, particularly if they have larger equipment such as wheelchairs.

Prepare thoroughly for any off-site visits
You will need to be thoroughly prepared when taking pupils out of school. If you are taking a large number of pupils on an outing or residential trip, the teacher responsible will need to check adult/pupil ratios, carry out risk assessments and also do a preliminary visit to look out for potential hazards.

Encouraging pupils to look out for risk themselves and being a good role model
Pupils should be aware that most activities carry some element of risk. Many children have little opportunity to be independent and to think and explore for themselves, which is an important part of growing up. When carrying out activities, talk to pupils about the kinds of risks which you are looking out for so that

they start to look for themselves. You should also show that you act safely yourself – pupils will take their lead from you and you should make sure that you do not act in a way which could be dangerous to others. Make sure you show through your own actions that you take safety seriously.

> pupils will take their lead from you

brilliant case study

Gina has just started a job in a new primary school. She is regularly on playground duty and notices that staff often carry cups of tea and coffee outside, particularly in colder weather. They are also able to take hot drinks to their classrooms. Gina is very alert to this as in her previous school there was an accident in which a pupil suffered serious burns after running into an adult who was carrying a hot drink. As she is new, she does not wish to appear to be a killjoy; however, she is anxious that the same thing does not happen again.

- Should Gina say anything?
- Can you think of a way in which this could be resolved without upsetting other staff?

Health and Safety at Work Act 1974

This act was designed to protect everyone at work through procedures for preventing accidents. Everyone in the workplace is required to observe the procedures below.

Reporting any hazards

All members of the school community should be alert to any hazards in school which might cause injury to themselves or others. The school is required to carry out an annual risk assessment to determine which areas and activities are most likely to be hazardous, the likelihood of specific hazards occurring and those who are at risk. Pupils and staff need to be vigilant and immediately report any hazards that they notice to the appropriate person. This may be the school's health and safety representative, the headteacher or another member of staff. You should be aware of the designated person to whom you should report health and safety matters.

Following the school's health and safety policy

The school has an obligation to have a health and safety policy which should give information to all staff about the procedures that the school has in place to ensure that it is as safe as possible. All new staff joining the school should be given induction training in safety procedures and what to do in case of emergencies.

brilliant dos and don'ts

Do

✔ Be vigilant at all times.

✔ Use and store equipment safely.

✔ Challenge any unidentified persons.

✔ Ensure you know the health and safety procedures in your school.

Don't

✘ Carry out any activities without being sure that they are safe.

✘ Ignore any hazards – report or remove immediately.

✘ Leave any hazardous materials within the reach of children.

Making sure that their actions do not harm themselves or others

All staff should ensure that any actions they take are not likely to harm or cause a danger to others in the school. This includes tidying up and putting things away after use. You must also consider the effects of not taking action; for example, if you discover a potential hazard you should not ignore it and it is your responsibility to report it as appropriate.

Using any safety equipment provided

If you carry out any activities with pupils which require you or they to use safety equipment such as tools or googles, this should always be used. In addition, if you are working with very young children, you may also need to use items like cupboard locks, safety gates, socket covers and window catches. You should always use manufacturers' guidelines when using equipment and it should be checked regularly. There should also be guidelines in the school's policy for the safe use and storage of equipment.

> ensure that pupils are cared for and safe at all times

All staff working in a school have a responsibility to ensure that pupils are cared for and safe at all times. The Children Act 1989 and Children (Scotland) Act 1995 also require that staff protect children from risks as far as possible when they are in their care.

brilliant activity

Risk assessments are required to be carried out prior to all school trips, journeys and residential activities. Find out the named person in your school for ensuring that these take place and what kinds of risks need to be documented. What then happens to the paperwork?

Responding to sickness, accidents and emergencies

Support staff will often be asked to be first aiders in schools and as a result will be on duty at breaks and lunchtimes to tend playground accidents or any sickness. If you are asked to do this you will need to be sent on first aid training which should be renewed every three years. You should not attempt to carry out any first aid or treat a casualty unless you have had the correct training – if you are the only adult in the vicinity you must make sure that you follow the correct procedures until help arrives. This should be a qualified first aider and, if necessary, an ambulance. You will need to support and reassure not only the casualty but also other pupils who may be present. Others may be distressed depending on what they have witnessed, or may be in shock themselves. Make sure that you and any others on the scene are not put at any unnecessary risk.

Following the incident you will also be required to fill in the school's documentation so that there is a record of any treatment which has been carried out. In some schools, particularly with younger pupils, you may need to phone parents or send home a brief note stating what treatment has been given. It is particularly important to tell parents if their child has had a bump on the head in case they suffer from any concussion. Accident forms will also need to be completed for any adults who are involved in accidents at work so that these are correctly documented.

Deer Lane Primary School Accident Report Form

Name of casualty ....

Exact location of incident...

Date and time ....

What was the injured person doing?...

How did the accident happen? ....

What injuries were sustained? ....

Treatment given..

Medical aid sought?...

Name of person dealing with incident...

Name of witness..

If the casualty was a child, at what time were parents informed?

....

Was hospital attended?..

....

Was the accident investigated?..

Signed...

Allergies and allergic reactions

In most schools there will be a number of pupils who have allergic reactions or intolerances to foods such as nuts, wheat or citrus fruits. All school staff should be aware of the identities of those pupils who have allergies, and clear instructions on how to deal with each case should be readily available. In particular, those on duty at lunchtimes or in extended school provision need to be kept informed, particularly if there are

> be aware of the identities of those pupils who have allergies

any changes or if new pupils arrive in school who have allergies. Staff should also be provided with training if they are asked to treat pupils who have allergies with epipens (used to treat anaphylactic shock and extreme allergic reactions). There may be a book or information folder for staff containing photos of relevant pupils, information about their allergies and contact telephone numbers. In some schools, photos and information may be displayed on staff room walls. However, care must always be taken to keep pupil information confidential.

Medicines and medical conditions

As well as allergies, there will be pupils in school who have medical conditions such as asthma, epilepsy or others which require medication to be administered. Any medication which is in school will usually be kept in the school office and, again, this should be documented so that it can be checked if necessary. Sometimes asthma pumps or epipens may also be kept in classrooms in case they are needed urgently.

Dealing with common illnesses

As you get to know the pupils with whom you work, it is likely that you will be able to identify times when they are not 'themselves' or are unwell. Remember that depending on their age or their needs, some pupils may not be able to communicate exactly what is wrong. General signs that children are 'off colour' could include:

- pale skin;
- flushed cheeks;
- rashes;
- different (quiet, clingy, irritable) behaviour;
- rings around the eyes;
- general fatigue.

Children will often develop symptoms more quickly than adults, as they may have less resistance to infection. Most schools will call parents or carers straight away if their child is showing signs or symptoms of illness. If children are on antibiotics, most schools will recommend that they stay off school until they have completed the course. The Department of Health has also issued a useful poster, 'Guidance on infection control in schools and nurseries', which could be displayed in the first aid area as a quick reference as it sets out some common illnesses and their characteristics.

Safeguarding

The term 'child protection' is increasingly being replaced by that of safeguarding. Safeguarding has been described as a broader definition of the range of ways in which adults and professionals who work with the child need to act when they are managing child protection issues. These are designed to prevent risk of harm to the welfare of children and young people rather than react to it. All adults have a responsibility to safeguard children and young people from harm – as professionals we have a duty to ensure that children and young people are protected whilst they are in our care. The kinds of issues to be considered in school policies should include:

- Pupils' physical health and safety and security whilst in school and on off-site visits.
- Pupils' safety when in the home environment.
- E-safety and security when using the internet.
- Partnership and involvement with other agencies.
- Staff awareness and school monitoring.

It is also important that pupils are aware of the boundaries of acceptable and unacceptable behaviour, both within and outside school. This means that they should know how to treat others and also know how they should expect to be treated. Pupils who are known to be on the 'at risk' register or those who have been identified as being at

> they should know how they should expect to be treated

greater risk should be supported by the school and outside agencies where appropriate. All agencies working with the pupil will need to be child-centred – for example, involving the pupil in meetings and asking for their opinion when discussing matters relating to them as much as possible.

↗ brilliant case study

Janine is working as a cover supervisor in Key Stage 3. She does not work with all the pupils as she tends to cover Maths and Music lessons, but this involves working with the same pupils each week. She has been approached by a pupil in Year 9 who has said that she is worried about her friend in her class whose father is an alcoholic – she says that her friend has confided in her that he is sometimes violent with both her and her mother.

● What should Janine do first?
● What should she say to the pupil?

Your local authority will have a local safeguarding children board (LSCB) which has been set up to ensure the safeguarding and welfare of children in your area. If your school does have a concern, the local authority will also act alongside it to follow guidelines and ensure that all agencies work together. The kinds of issues which may arise in schools will vary – however, you should always be alert to any safeguarding concerns and ensure that you are acting appropriately and within the correct guidelines.

Other agencies your school may deal with are:

● social services;
● NSPCC;
● health visitors;
● GP;

- probation service;
- police;
- psychology service.

---

brilliant example

Find a copy of your school's child protection or safeguarding policy. What measures does the school have in place for monitoring safeguarding issues?

When you are with pupils in school in any context, and particularly if you are on your own, you should also think about your own working so that both you and pupils are protected. The kinds of issues you should think about are shown in Figure 9.1.

Figure 9.1 Safe working

Physical contact

You may rightly have concerns about any physical contact with children or young people; however, in some situations it is appropriate to put an arm around a child if, for example, they are distressed or have hurt themselves. Young children can also often be demonstrative and will hug adults spontaneously. As a general rule you should always act sensibly and behave reactively rather than initiating any physical contact with pupils, and in particular ensure that you do not have any physical contact with pupils if there is nobody else around. There are some situations in which this is not possible; for example, if you are working with a pupil who has special educational needs and need to attend to their personal care. Make sure that you follow school policy at all times when doing this.

> **act sensibly and behave reactively**

brilliant tip

If you are in any doubt about whether or not you should have any physical contact with a pupil, it is always better not to.

Sharing concerns

You must always report any concerns, whether this is based on what a pupil has said or because you have observed something, and record what has happened. In this way you will also be protected if any further incidents occur. You should also inform managers if you have any concerns about other members of staff due to poor practice.

Propriety and behaviour

In your capacity as a professional working in a school, you should ensure that you act in a professional manner at all times. When working with pupils we are required to behave in an appropriate way and with respect for others, and to make sure that children and young people also understand what is expected of them. As adults we are also role models and so should set an example through our own behaviour.

Types and possible signs of abuse

You should always be alert to any signs that a pupil is the victim of abuse – these might include both physical and behavioural changes. The four main types of abuse are described below.

Physical

This involves being physically hurt or injured. Children and young people may suffer physical abuse on a persistent or spasmodic basis. If you notice any frequent signs of injury, such as regular bruises, burns or cuts, it is important to take action or investigate further. Less obvious signs of physical abuse may include fear of physical contact with others, reluctance to get changed for PE or sports sessions, or wanting to stay covered even in hot weather.

Emotional

Emotional abuse which is carried out by adults can involve the pupil continuously being 'put down' and criticised, as well as name calling and humiliation. The signs are that a pupil may become withdrawn or lack confidence, show regression or be 'clingy' towards adults, and have low self-esteem. Pupils who suffer from emotional abuse are more likely to be anxious about new situations and may appear distracted and unable to concentrate.

Sexual

This involves an adult or young person using a child sexually – for example, by touching their bodies inappropriately or by forcing them to look at sexual images or have sex. Signs to look out for may include sexual behaviour which is inappropriate to the child's age, genital irritation, clinginess or changes in the pupil's behaviour, appearing withdrawn or lacking trust in adults. Sexual abuse can be very difficult to identify and its signs may also indicate other kinds of abuse.

Neglect

This type of abuse means that the child or young person is not having their basic needs met by parents or carers. These basic needs include shelter, food, general hygiene, love and medical care. The signs of neglect may be that pupils are dirty, hungry, attention-seeking or generally failing to thrive.

Bullying

Although neglect will be caused by the child or young person's parent or carer, other other types of abuse may also be inflicted by their peers. One type of bullying which has become prevalent with the increased use of the internet and texting is cyber-bullying. This can be very unpleasant and schools are increasingly speaking to children and young people and their parents about being vigilant when using phones and the internet.

As a teaching assistant you are well placed to notice changes in pupils' behaviour or other possible signs of abuse. If you are at all concerned, make sure you speak to your school's child protection or safeguarding officer straight away. They will follow school policy and if necessary report to the local authority. Always keep a note of what happened, what you reported and who you told.

> you are well placed to notice changes in pupils' behaviour

brilliant recap

- Be vigilant at all times for any dangers to others' safety and security.
- Check the environment as well as equipment as a matter of course.
- Be aware of your school's health and safety and safeguarding policies.

- Make sure you have had any training if you are asked to administer first aid.
- Follow up on any concerns.
- Always look out for any signs of abuse and report immediately.

Further reading

- www.bbc.co.uk/health/treatments/first_aid/index.shtml – Guide to First Aid.
- www.hse.gov.uk – Health and Safety Executive.
- www.kidscape.org.uk – A charity to prevent bullying and child abuse.
- www.ceop.gov.uk – Child Exploitation and Online Protection Centre, an organisation which aims to provide information to parents, children and education professionals around safety online.
- www.nspcc.org.uk – NSPCC's website.
- www.anti-bullyingalliancetoolkit.org.uk – Guidance and practical ideas to help tackle bullying.
- www.cyberbullying.co.uk – Advice on what to do for anyone bullied by text, email, web, etc.

CHAPTER 10

Extended and out of school provision

More and more, teaching assistants are supporting and leading sessions during out of school clubs, extended hours provision and other activities which may take place inside or outside school hours. Although it should not be a requirement of your role, the kinds of opportunities which running these activities provide could be good for your own personal and professional development and raise your profile both within the school and also the wider community. You may also regularly assist on school journeys or trips and need to be mindful of various school and legal requirements. In these contexts you may also liaise more with families; this chapter will look at the role of the family support worker and how they provide valuable links between schools and communities. We will look at some different examples of how you might support pupils as well as other staff in this wider context and how to manage different activities and situations.

Breakfast and after-school club

Breakfast and after-school clubs are now part of the day in many primary schools. They were developed as part of the extended schools agenda which followed the introduction of Every Child Matters and the Children Act in 2004. They became known as 'wrap around childcare' in some authorities and have enabled parents of primary school aged children to leave them on site from early in the morning before the start of school until early in the evening, depending on their requirements. They are also able to select the days and times which are best for them, although the provision will often have waiting lists as the costs are reduced by government subsidies. The development of breakfast and after school clubs has meant that many school sites are open for longer and will also offer other clubs to pupils if they have the staff or facilities.

Breakfast and after school clubs may be run by an external organisation or individual on the school site, although they may also be run by or employ existing support staff. They are also required to fulfil OFSTED criteria as well as being liable for inspection. It is likely that they will provide meals and snacks for pupils and also run a range of activities within the space and time available. If you are part of breakfast or after-school provision your role will follow the principles of playwork (a profession which sets out to enrich children's play without the need to be driven by education or care requirements) and will be different from that which you have during the day: you are likely to be working with groups of children and carrying out creative or recreational activities with them rather than supporting teaching and learning. However, in some schools there may also be additional support with homework during these times if there is a quiet area that the children can use as well as staff availability.

> your role will follow the principles of playwork

brilliant example

Migena works at a large primary school. During the day she works in Years 5 and 6 but before school starts she works in the breakfast club which provides childcare for pupils whose parents need this additional facility. Migena runs some play and creative activities for the children and also gives them breakfast alongside the breakfast club co-ordinator. Sometimes children in the club will have school duties such as taking round the registers before the start of school and Migena ensures that everyone has a chance to do this regularly.

Extra-curricular activities

If you are providing extra-curricular activities, you may be supporting or leading extended hours provision in the form of clubs or organised sessions which pupils attend in your school on a daily or weekly basis. Depending on your responsibilities, you may be asked to plan activities yourself for pupils or to work with others to do this. The kinds of activities which take place as part of extended school provision will vary from school to school and depend on the age and needs of pupils. They may include the following:

- play and recreational activities;
- fitness classes;
- drama;
- sport;
- musical activities;
- study support;
- arts, crafts and other special interest clubs;
- volunteering and business and enterprise activities;
- Duke of Edinburgh Award scheme.

brilliant examples

Tom works in a secondary school as a learning support assistant for a pupil in Year 9. He has an interest in basketball and is a qualified coach, and has just started to run a basketball club on Mondays after school for pupils in Years 7 and 8.

▶

Lucy works in Year 2 with a teacher who is the school's Music co-ordinator. As she is a competent pianist she has asked the teacher whether she can develop her skills and extend herself professionally by getting more involved with music in the school. She has accompanied the Key Stage 1 and 2 choirs on several occasions and helps with the rehearsals during lunchtime once a week.

These kinds of extra activities will give pupils the opportunity to try out tasks and activities which they may not otherwise have the chance to, and also encourage them to try new things and extend their skills and knowledge. You may find that some pupils in your school are enthusiastic about trying as many as they can, whilst others may not join any. There may also be some activities which are more popular than others and the school may need to review the kinds of activities which are on offer depending on the resources available.

Although you may be supporting a teacher or another colleague in delivering extra-curricular activities, if you are in sole charge you will have a number of additional responsibilities and will need to bear these in mind.

Health and safety

Observing health and safety law is a requirement of which you will need to be fully aware. As well as knowing your school's health and safety policy (see Chapter 9) you will also have additional responsibility during the session for ensuring that pupils are aware of what to do in case they need to evacuate the building, making sure that they behave safely at all times and encouraging them to think about safety when carrying out activities. You will also need to know about any health needs of the pupils (for example, asthma or any allergies) in case they need access to medication whilst they are in your care.

Safe removal, use and storage of equipment

Make sure before you start to run your activity that you have checked any equipment which is required and are able to access it at the time it is needed. You may need to take it through another room which is being used by others, or have to remove it from locked cupboards or storage rooms. Make sure you have enough for the number of pupils who will be attending and whether they need to bring kit or additional items – if necessary write a letter to parents and carers outlining what will be required. Following the activity you will need to replace any school equipment and make sure that it is stored safely and securely.

Making sure you set clear ground rules for behaviour

You will need to make a point of doing this so that the group are clear on what they are expected to do and know the rules of the activity. This is especially important if you are using tools or equipment but you should do it in every instance so that pupils are clear from the outset (see also Chapter 4).

Keeping registers or logs of attendance

You should always ensure that you comply with the school's regulations for checking attendance. You should have been provided with a list or register of names so that you know who is present and can sign pupils in at the start and out at the end. Even if you think that you know exactly who has arrived, it is very easy for one person to be missed, and you will be accountable for each pupil who is present. You will also need to be very clear about collection arrangements and who has left at the end of the activity.

brilliant dos and don'ts

Do

✔ Before you start the club, find out whether the activity is something that the pupils will be interested in doing.

✔ Take time to plan and think about the format.

✔ Emphasise the importance of good behaviour and timekeeping.

✔ Make sure you give pupils the opportunity to evaluate the activity and give their own suggestions.

Don't

✘ Put yourself forward unless you are able to be there every week – it is important not to let pupils down.

✘ Compromise on safety.

✘ Forget to check any tools or equipment regularly.

brilliant tip

If you are thinking of offering to run a club or activity because you have an interest or would like to extend your experience, go and observe and support a colleague in your school first and make a note of the kinds of things which they need to do in addition to organising the pupils and their activities.

brilliant case study

Saskia is an experienced support assistant and in addition has just started to run a small craft club for Key Stage 2 after school. She has the use of a classroom and has a group of 12 children for the activities. Saskia has taken a register of pupils at the beginning so knows who is present but, following the club, one of the Year 6 children tells her that she is allowed to walk home on her own. Ten minutes later her mother comes to collect her and although she is late tells Saskia that she did not give her permission to walk home alone and will be speaking to the headteacher straight away.

● How should Saskia have responded to the girl's request?

● What should she do now to support the parent?

Further extended school provision

Although these kinds of clubs and extra-curricular activities have always been available to pupils, they are not the only aspect of extended services which schools may now be expected to offer. The Every Child Matters programme was introduced nationally in 2004 to increase the support available through children's services so that all children and young people would have access to more opportunities. Services are now encouraged and expected to work together rather than in isolation so that any issues are picked up earlier. Every Child Matters focuses on five key outcomes for children:

● to be healthy;

● to stay safe;

● to enjoy and achieve;

● to make a positive contribution;

● to achieve economic wellbeing.

Since the profile of extended schools has been raised, schools have been developing their resources and widening their remit so that they are able to work alongside others to do this. The extended schools programme was introduced to develop the kinds of facilities which are on offer to pupils and

> schools have been developing their resources

their families in both primary and secondary schools and develop community cohesion. After consultation with families and involving them in discussion about the kinds of services which would benefit the community, schools and local authorities have introduced a range of provision catering for different needs. These will be based in different schools in the area according to the requirements of the community and the facilities which are available in each; for example, some schools have their own swimming pools or others their own athletics track. In primary schools extended services have tended to focus around childcare and additional extra-curricular activities although additional services such as parenting support and other courses may also be available through outside organisations. In secondary schools, the aim has been to develop provision so that they will offer both curriculum-based and additional courses such as first aid or ICT for pupils and the wider community. They may also work with young people on community projects and voluntary work, and in some cases work with local primary schools through activities such as reading support. Working with local authorities, many schools will now also provide facilities or additional services for pupils in other schools and for the wider community through working in cluster groups to deliver co-ordinated provision. The kinds of organisations which may be involved within the community are as follows.

Adult education services

Adult education may be able to offer classes and additional training to young people and to parents. In some cases creative, English language or educational classes are offered for parents alongside their children. This can also have benefits for those parents who may see schools as threatening or who have had bad experiences themselves, encouraging them to have more confidence to have contact with schools.

▶ brilliant example

Callie runs an art group for children and their parents as part of the extended schools programme. As well as working as a learning support assistant three days per week, she is an art teacher for the local adult education group. She has been able to work with her school to set up and run the group using some of the school's resources and this has encouraged many parents to become more involved with the school as well as developing good relationships and learning alongside their children.

Health and social care services

The range of services which are required at some stage by children and young people are diverse. They may include the input of professionals such as speech and language therapists, behavioural support services, or occupational and physiotherapists. In some cases, special schools in communities may be able to offer wider access to these kinds of services for all pupils through creating more streamlined support services.

All schools are being encouraged to work towards achieving healthy schools status, which requires them to meet a number of criteria in areas such as physical activity, healthy eating and emotional wellbeing and this should also be supported by the extended schools programme.

Children's centres

Many existing children's centres offer wider services including health and family support and referral. In some cases children's centres are being linked directly to schools, which is more straightforward for both children and parents as it will mean that pupils' childcare and school experience will be on one site.

Although these additional services are based in schools, the expectation is that they will not be run by existing teachers. Support staff, volunteers and professions within the wider community should all be involved in providing the kinds of services which are needed and you may have the opportunity to contribute in some way. Parents should also be involved at every level in making sure that the kinds of services which are on offer are a reflection of what is needed within the community. It is important for the success of the programme that parents are encouraged to contribute ideas and become involved in the development of extended schools as much as possible.

> you may have the opportunity to contribute

brilliant activity

Find out about the kind of extended school provision which is available both through your own school and in your local cluster group or family of schools. If necessary, you may be able to find out through your local authority about what is available.

brilliant case study

James runs the local scout group and the venue he has been using has just told him that they will be unable to carry on using it due to building work over the next few months. As he also works at the local secondary school as a member of support staff, he has had the idea of booking the school hall and also offering Duke of Edinburgh award training to pupils from the surrounding area as an extra activity.

● Would James be able to do this?

● Where might he go for support in order to see his idea through?

The role of family support workers

The family support worker was originally only accessed through social worker and counselling services. However, due to the extended schools agenda, education family support workers have developed in recent years to form a school-based link between schools and families that is closer and more productive. Family support workers are often allocated some time within their day to spend talking to parents and families and developing closer links where these are needed. They support parents and pupils and can provide an informal but often much needed ear, which can be perceived as less threatening than speaking to a member of teaching staff. Family support workers will also liaise with parents to develop additional extended school provision where this is needed, or to advise and support them if further services are required. In many cases they will work with parents to support pupils who are having difficulties at school and try to enable them to overcome any barriers which they are facing.

If you are working as a family support worker as part of your role within school, you should have been offered additional training and support. The role can often be similar to that of a counsellor and you will need to be a good listener as well as being able to relate well to others. If you have additional skills such as speaking a second language, especially if it is one spoken by large numbers of parents, this will be particularly useful. You will need to be available at the beginning and end of the day when parents may be on site, although they should also be able to make appointments to see you if they need more time.

> you will need to be a good listener

brilliant tip

If you are working as a family support worker, make sure that your school newsletter or website regularly reminds families that you are there, or that the school noticeboard gives this information – it is often the case that parents and carers will not remember that you are there until they need you.

Taking pupils on school trips

It is important for all pupils to have the opportunity to explore different environments both through the provision of outdoor learning environments and through having access to school trips and journeys. Support staff will regularly be asked to assist on school trips, especially if they have an additional skill such as being a first aider. If you support an individual pupil it will also be part of your role to go with them and support them. Depending on the age of pupils and the purpose of the trip, it may also involve taking part in additional activities. You will need to be particularly aware of safety when taking pupils out of school; if you are taking a large number of pupils on an outing or residential trip, the trip organiser should carry out a risk assessment beforehand. This means that they will check what kinds of risks there might be during the trip and the likelihood of it occurring. The level of risk may depend on a number of factors:

- the adult/pupil ratio;
- where you are going;
- the activities the pupils will be undertaking;
- transport to the venue and back.

Risk assessment comprises of assessing the level of risk in each instance and then filling in a form to show what action will be taken to avoid this occurring.

The facilities will need to be checked to make sure that they are adequate for the needs of the pupils; for example, if you are taking a large number of children or young people, or a pupil who has a disability. As well as a risk assessment, preparations need to include other considerations. A trip should always be planned thoroughly so that the adults are prepared for whatever happens. Preparations include the need to:

> a trip should always be planned thoroughly

- seek and gain parental consent;
- arrange for suitable safe transport;
- take a first aid kit and first aider as well as inhalers or medication for pupils who may need them;
- take appropriate clothing for the activity or weather;
- make lists of adults and the pupils for whom they will be responsible;
- give information sheets to all helpers, including timings and any safety information;
- make sure pupils you may have concerns about are in your group rather than with a volunteer helper.

As a member of support staff you will not be responsible for making all of these checks, but it is helpful to be aware of them so that you can ask the teacher who is organising the trip if anything is not clear.

brilliant dos and don'ts

Do

✔ Make sure you are thoroughly prepared before the day and have everything ready.

✔ Check that you are aware of the health needs of pupils in your group and have any medication with you.

✔ Offer support to any parents or volunteers who may not have been on a trip before.

✔ Remember any time constraints when you are out.

Don't

✘ Take anything into your own hands without informing the trip co-ordinator.

✘ Relax – you are in a position of responsibility at all times!

✘ Forget that the younger the children, the less they will be aware of safety issues.

brilliant recap

● Extended schools will vary according to the needs of the community.

● They may take the form of additional clubs and activities as well as wider provision.

● You should not have to carry out extended school duties as part of your role but it may be a valuable form of professional development.

Further reading

The TDA website has a range of suggestions and links to publications which may be of benefit to those running extended school provision in a variety of contexts:

● www.tda.gov.uk

● www.teachernet.gov.uk/extendedschools

● www.dcsf.gov.uk/everychildmatters

CHAPTER 11

Reflecting on your practice and continuing professional development

The role of the teaching assistant has changed dramatically over the last 10 to 15 years. It has been 'professionalised' as the number of support staff has risen and there is now a huge range of roles and responsibilities within schools. This chapter will look at the importance of reflecting on your own practice and considering your continuing professional development (CPD) through the appraisal process. It will include looking at how you can keep up to date with career developments, as well as national and local requirements which are regularly updated. This will also put you in a stronger position when applying for different jobs within the sector. It is important to know how to approach looking for new jobs, writing your CV and going to interviews. Finally, you should think about different ways in which you can manage a work/life balance, particularly if you have a family of your own.

Continuing professional development and the appraisal process

Teaching assistants are increasingly part of the whole school staff appraisal process. This means that in the same way that teachers need to review their performance each year and look at targets to work towards, teaching assistants will be asked to meet their line manager to do the same thing. This should not be seen as threatening and is designed to support you in thinking about what you do and how you carry out reflective practice (see Figure 11.1 overleaf).

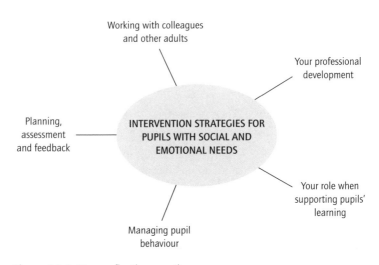

Figure 11.1 Your reflective practice

Reflective practice is the process of looking at your own professional actions and thinking about ways in which you might set goals in order to change or improve your practice. As part of the appraisal process, it is an opportunity to discuss and evaluate your role and to consider the kinds of changes that could be made. It relates not only to your professional development but also to how you carry out individual activities with pupils and to other aspects of your role. You need to reflect on a regular basis and should have the opportunity to discuss your thoughts and your ideas with your colleagues; in this way you will be able to identify areas of strength as well as exploring those which may need further development. Support staff will often have quite diverse roles in schools and inevitably you will find that you are more confident in some areas than in others; by reflecting on your practice and how you work with your colleagues you will become more effective in your role and gain confidence.

> you need to reflect on a regular basis

brilliant example

Tamsin has been working within the same year group (Y1) for several years. She enjoys her work, gets on well with the class teacher and feels quite confident in her work. The school has just introduced performance management for teaching assistants and, as part of this process, she reflects on her knowledge and skills. As a consequence she goes on a training course to update her ICT skills. Although she had not considered this before her appraisal, following the course she is much more confident and is able to use ICT more in her practice with pupils.

When carrying out reflective practice as part of the appraisal process, you should have the opportunity to consider different aspects of your role prior to any meeting with your line manager. You may wish to use the headings in the spider diagram above/opposite in order to help you to gather ideas. In this way you will be more prepared for the meeting and able to put your suggestions forward.

Your professional development

As you are employed as a professional, you should be able to think about your role on a regular basis. This means looking at your own job description and thinking about different areas of development. It might be helpful to consider different ways in which you can extend your knowledge and try new things.

Your role when supporting pupils' learning

You should take some time to look at different activities which you have carried out with individuals or groups of pupils and evaluate how the sessions went. However experienced you are, you should always consider different ways of approaching teaching and learning activities. It may also be helpful for your line manager or another colleague to observe you working with pupils as part of your appraisal so that they can also help you to evaluate your practice.

Managing pupil behaviour

This can be one of the more challenging aspects of your work. You will need to work as part of a whole school approach to behaviour management which should set out the kinds of sanctions and strategies you are able to use with pupils. In order to manage behaviour effectively you will need to be firm and consistent with pupils so that they understand boundaries and are aware of the consequences of their actions (for more on behaviour management, see Chapter 4).

Planning, assessment and feedback

You may or may not be involved in the planning process, but it is important that you know what it involves and that you have some opportunity to give feedback to teachers following learning activities. As your role is supporting teaching and learning, your feedback will inform the next cycle of planning. Make sure you know:

● the learning objectives for each session;

● whether any of the pupils have particular targets to work on;

● pupils' backgrounds and circumstances which may affect their behaviour or learning;

- how you will feed back to the teacher (is this written or verbal, at a set time or planned?).

As part of your performance management, reflect on how much you are involved in different aspects of planning, assessment and feedback and whether this could be improved.

Working with colleagues and other adults

Your relationships with your colleagues are important as communication is a key part of your work with pupils. Think about how you relate to others in your school and the support you offer them within various teams you may belong to (year group, subject area, class, key stage). If you support a pupil who has special educational needs, you may also work with teams of professionals who are external to the school, such

> think about how you relate to others

as educational psychologists or speech therapists. It is also likely that you will work with parents and carers, particularly if you work closely with one pupil. When considering this aspect of your role you should think about the ways in which you can develop your relationships with others so that pupils are supported more effectively.

brilliant dos and don'ts

Do

✔ Be honest with yourself and others.
✔ Think about all aspects of your work.
✔ Include both successes and failures.
✔ Ask a colleague for help if you need it.

Don't

✘ Worry about your appraisal – it is meant to help you in your role.

✗　Forget that all members of staff, including the headteacher, will go through the same process.

✗　Try to develop everything at once – your targets will need to be achievable.

Following this preparation, you will set a date for your initial appraisal meeting with your line manager or the member of staff who is responsible for teaching assistants in the school. This may, for example, be the deputy head or the SENCO if you are an individual support assistant. The structure of the meeting will depend on your own school's approach but it is likely that you will consider your job description in the light of what you do on a day-to-day basis and think about whether it is still a reflection of your role. You may then talk through your classroom observation if you have had one, and think about any issues which have come up as a result of this. Finally, you might discuss the aspects of your job which give you the most and least satisfaction and think about any additional training which you would find helpful following your reflection on your role. You will then think about three or four targets to work on over the next 12 months. These targets should partly comprise of any training which you will be doing anyway, such as attending a safeguarding course as part of the school staff, or completing your certificate in supporting teaching and learning.

brilliant tip

Make sure your targets are SMART:

● 　Specific: Ensure your target says exactly what is required.

● 　Measurable: Make sure you can measure whether the target has been achieved.

● 　Achievable: The target should not be inaccessible or too difficult.

- Realistic: Ensure you have access to the training or resources that may be required.
- Time-bound: There should be a limit to the time you have available to achieve your target. This is because otherwise you may continually put it off to another date!

The main points of your conversation will then be documented by your line manager and then the targets recorded in a format such as the one below.

Professional Review Meeting

Name .... Date ....

Line manager..

Areas discussed ....

Review of last year's targets (if applicable):

New targets for professional development:

1

2

3

To be reviewed on:

Signed .... (TA)

Signed .... (Line manager)

Keeping up to date with career developments

You will usually be able to keep up with the kinds of courses and development opportunities which are available to support staff through your school. You may find that the school invites people from different outside agencies to speak to or train staff and these may be optional or obligatory for support staff. Your line manager or supervisor should be able to give you advice and information about training and help you to decide on the best courses or meetings to attend. Additionally, your SENCO may be able to give you details of any courses to support your work with pupils who have special educational needs. If you have any difficulty finding help, your local education authority will publish details of courses well in advance and these should be available through your local teacher development centre. You should also keep up to date through reading educational publications or websites such as the *TES*, or those specifically for teaching assistants such as *Learning Support* magazine.

brilliant case study

Jackie is working as an individual support assistant for a blind pupil in a secondary school. She has been there for two years and, although she is very experienced and well trained for her work with the pupil, she does not have any qualifications. She has been investigating some of her options – she would like to be better qualified as there is a possibility that her pupil may be moving schools. However, she does not have much contact with her line manager as she is not full time, and there are no points of contact during the week.

● What should Jackie do first?

● Is there anything else she could do if the school could not support her request?

Over the past few years there have been many developments in the qualifications and courses available for support staff, through NVQs, DCSF induction training, HLTA, foundation degrees and Support Work in Schools (SWIS). At the time of writing, the qualifications are being reviewed and award, certificate and diplomas being developed in supporting teaching and learning. There is also some confusion about different levels and whether there should be a pay scale for support staff as pay and conditions vary between local authorities.

The training and development agency website (www.tda.gov. uk) gives guidance and recommendations for most support staff qualifications and what the different levels mean nationally, as currently different local authorities may give assistants different job titles to reflect their level of experience or expertise. For example, in some LAs, support staff with little or no experience or who mainly deal with photocopying, displays and so on may be called classroom assistants, whereas those who are more involved with supporting teaching and learning are teaching assistants. This is not, however, a national requirement.

It is important when looking at qualifications to have good advice and to choose the right one for you because many of them are work based and so will give a good indication of the level at which you are working. If you can, ask others about courses that they have been on so that you can find out which most appeal or may be useful to you. Courses may be full or part time and, depending on your hours at school, you may have to speak to your headteacher for time out in order to study. Alternatively, some centres offer evening courses so that you can attend outside school hours.

> ask others about courses that they have been on

> ☀ **brilliant** tip
>
> Always keep a record of all courses you attend and qualifications gained. They will be a good record of your professional development and will be useful for you to have at hand if you need to update your CV or attend an interview.

Making a job application

Whatever your role, it is likely that at some stage you will need to think about changing your job. It can be fairly daunting to do this, particularly if you have been in the same school for some time. In many cases, teaching assistants have started their careers by volunteering in their own child's school and gradually building up their role and experience and may feel disloyal or lack confidence in looking elsewhere. However, you may have more experience than you think and if you have been on additional training or have developed areas of speciality, you may find that it is appealing to consider working in another school or even changing key stages.

you may have more experience than you think

Before you even apply to a different school, find out as much about it as you can and visit it if possible. You should make sure that you check the advertisement or person specification to ensure that you have the required experience or qualifications if necessary. It is likely that you will need to give the names of references – one of these should always be your current headteacher so you will need to check with them first.

brilliant tip

Having an up-to-date CV which you revise every year or so can be a useful additional document to have to hand if needed when considering a new role.

Writing a CV or filling in an application form?

When making an application, you will find that some advertisements will ask you to fill in a form, whereas others may ask you to send your CV with a covering letter. You will need to make sure that you do this carefully, particularly if the school specifies that it should be handwritten – never write straight onto the form without making a draft first. Your supporting statement or covering letter will need to be well written and show how you fulfil the requirements of the person specification. You should use it to sell yourself and to say why you are the best person for the post, so include details such as relevant previous experience, additional training you may have attended, or specific areas of expertise.

If you are writing a CV you should always include a number of essential details:

- name;
- address;
- other contact details (email, phone numbers);
- date of birth;
- qualifications;
- employment history (start with your most recent employer and make sure any gaps in employment are explained, for example, having children, travel, etc.);
- other interests and relevant experiences (running a scout group or Duke of Edinburgh award, first aider, guitar player, etc.).

brilliant tip

Always ask another person to check through your application and supporting statement for you before sending them.

Going to interviews

Going to an interview will always be a useful experience and you should try to view it as such, even if you are nervous. Remember that as well as the school finding out if you would be the right person for the post, you are also finding out about whether the school is right for you. Try to give yourself plenty of time to arrive and dress comfortably without being too casual or overly confident. Remember that first impressions will be part of the process!

There are some key questions which you may be asked – try to be prepared by having some answers ready in advance. You may also be able to ask other assistants in your school for the kinds of questions which they have been asked at interviews.

brilliant example

The types of questions you may be asked include:

- Why have you applied for this role?
- What kind of experience have you had?
- What have been your most/least satisfying experiences in the classroom?
- What would you do if a parent approached you with a question about their child's progress?
- Outline different examples of how you might promote a pupil's independence in the classroom.
- How should you approach the management of pupil behaviour?

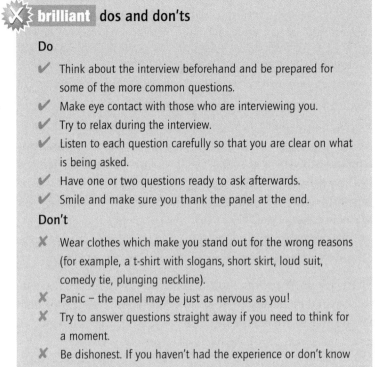

brilliant dos and don'ts

Do

✔ Think about the interview beforehand and be prepared for some of the more common questions.

✔ Make eye contact with those who are interviewing you.

✔ Try to relax during the interview.

✔ Listen to each question carefully so that you are clear on what is being asked.

✔ Have one or two questions ready to ask afterwards.

✔ Smile and make sure you thank the panel at the end.

Don't

✘ Wear clothes which make you stand out for the wrong reasons (for example, a t-shirt with slogans, short skirt, loud suit, comedy tie, plunging neckline).

✘ Panic – the panel may be just as nervous as you!

✘ Try to answer questions straight away if you need to think for a moment.

✘ Be dishonest. If you haven't had the experience or don't know the answer, say so.

Maintaining a work/life balance

One of the more challenging aspects of your role can be maintaining a work/life balance. You may have started part time and been asked to increase your hours, or have just returned to work after having a family. There will always be times when it can seem difficult to juggle your different roles; this can be exacerbated if you decide to go on additional training,

> it can seem difficult to juggle your different roles

particularly if this takes place over several months. It can sometimes seem as though everything happens at once, for example if you have started a new job while one of your own children has just started secondary school. However, many teaching assistants and other support staff are in a similar position, often as single parents or with other additional pressures, and there are some ways in which you can plan and use your time more effectively.

Plan to have some 'you time' each week

You should make sure that even if this is just for a couple of hours, you have some time away from being Mum/Dad/TA/ student so that you have something to look forward to, whether this is a hobby or socialising with friends.

Plan your time carefully

You may need to review how you use your time – this may mean sorting out meals a week in advance, having your groceries delivered, or allocating housework to specific days of the week. People with less time often seem to manage to do more through careful time management.

Make the most of any offers of help or arrange some swaps with friends

If you have friends with children of a similar age, arrange some childcare swaps so that you get more time to yourself if possible.

Speak to your own family and enlist their help

Even if each person has one responsibility each week this will mean that you have less to do.

Join any TA forums or networks

This may help you with any study you are doing and can also help you to feel that you are not alone.

Whilst there will always be times in which you may feel that there are not enough hours in the day, your work with pupils should give you plenty of job satisfaction and be very rewarding. There are also many more opportunities for you now as the role of the teaching assistant develops to extend your skills and expertise and you may decide to take your career in a different direction through your experiences.

 brilliant recap

- Prepare carefully for your appraisal through careful reflection.
- Try to keep up to date by reading educational publications and looking online.
- Keep finding ways to extend yourself as part of your role.
- Make sure your CV and record of professional development is up to date.
- Prepare carefully for interviews.
- Try to actively maintain a good work/life balance.

Further reading

- www.learningsupport.co.uk – magazine for teaching assistants in primary schools.
- www.tes.co.uk – *The Times Educational Supplement*.
- www.napta.org.uk – National Association of Professional Teaching Assistants.
- www.tda.gov.uk – Standards site for teaching assistants.
- www.teachernet.gov.uk/teachingassistants – useful information for support staff.

Unions for teaching assistants

- www.unison.org.uk – Unison.
- www.gmb.org.uk – GMB.
- www.unitetheunion.org – Unite.

Appendix 1: Case study solutions

Chapter 1

⟋ brilliant case study

Emma has just spent break talking to Lorraine, who is another teaching assistant working in Key Stage 2. She has found some challenges in her work with a particular pupil in the class that Lorraine supported the previous year. Lorraine is able to talk through some of the strategies which worked and which she may find useful.

● In what ways will this chat be useful?

● How else might Lorraine be able to help Emma in the long term?

Solution

This chat will be useful as another teaching assistant will be fully aware of the kinds of challenges which Emma is facing. As well as having more time than the teacher, Lorraine will be able to understand how to deal with the pupil from the same point of view and it will be more helpful for Emma to hear her talking about what she found worked best. She may also be able to help by discussing how she worked with the teacher when supporting the child.

 **brilliant** case study

Sina works in a small village primary school as a teaching assistant in Year 2. Her child is in another class and her best friend is also a parent at the school. Sina's friend regularly tries to find out what happens in the class on a daily basis and often questions her on the way home about specific children. She is also very keen that her child is put up to the next level in reading and asks Sina to 'sort it out' for her.

- What should Sina do in this situation?
- Why is it important that she does not talk to her friend about what happens in class?

Solution

It is very important that Sina explains to her friend that she has a responsibility for confidentiality as part of her role within the school and that it is not appropriate to discuss other children with her. She is taking advantage of her relationship of Sina but also putting her in a very difficult position and jeopardising her job. Playgrounds are often the place where rumours and gossip start and Sina should not be made a part of this. In addition, if Sina's friend is not happy with her child's progress it should be pointed out to her that she should make an appointment with the class teacher. If her friend persists Sina should seek advice and further support from her line manager.

Chapter 2

 **brilliant** case study

Lulu is working in a small one form entry primary school and usually floats between Years 1 and 2. The teaching assistant who has worked in the reception class for the last few years has gone on maternity leave and, as cover is needed, Lulu has been asked to step in for a few months. She does not have experience of the EYFS and soon starts to feel that she needs more support.

● Where should Lulu go for support in the first instance?
● Is there anywhere else Lulu could seek help?

Solution

Lulu should go either to her line manager or to the Foundation Stage manager and talk through her concerns as soon as possible, particularly if she is anxious about fulfilling her role correctly. She should not wait until her appraisal or until the subject comes up as part of her professional development as this may not happen for some time. If she is not successful in approaching either of these individuals, Lulu may wish to speak to the deputy head or seek advice from colleagues who may have worked with this age group. Early Years advisors within the local authority may be able to give information about training dates on the EYFS for assistants.

🔍 brilliant case study

Tina has just got a job supporting a reception teacher working in a small school. In her first job as a teaching assistant, she was at a larger primary where the reception and nursery classes worked together as a unit for the Foundation Stage and did not have much contact with the rest of the school, particularly as they were housed in a separate building. In her new job, the school does not have a nursery, and the reception class are expected to join in far more with whole school activities such as assemblies. Tina is surprised by the difference and is quite unsettled as a result as she is not sure that it is appropriate for this age group.

▶

● Do you think that this could be a problem?

● Should Tina say anything?

Solution

This could be a problem if Tina starts to voice her concerns to others in the school rather than speaking to the Foundation Stage manager or another member of the senior management team (SMT). She should speak to her line manager for her own peace of mind and for reassurance in the first instance rather than saying anything negative to colleagues. She should remember that every school will be slightly different and that the headteacher should be aware of the Foundation Stage requirements and will have reasons for managing whole school activities in the way in which he or she has.

brilliant case study

Alistair is an experienced teaching assistant who is working with a newly qualified teacher in Year 5. They have been working well throughout the autumn term and the teacher sends Alistair her plans each week in advance. However, on looking through the Maths plans for the following week, Alistair has noticed that she is aiming to deliver an ambitious lesson to the group which he knows that some of the pupils he supports are going to struggle with.

● Should Alistair say something and, if so, what?

● How can this situation be managed sensitively if these kinds of issues continue?

Solution

Alistair should definitely say something but will need to approach this situation sensitively so as not to undermine the teacher. He could try something like, 'I worked on this with these children in Year 4 and they had a lot of difficulty understanding the concept – would it be worth taking them back over what we did last year first?'

Alistair's teacher will be working closely with a mentor as she is newly qualified, so if these kinds of issues continue it is likely that they will become apparent as the year goes on and be managed appropriately.

brilliant case study

Sinem has been asked to work within the Biology department at her school as there are not enough support staff for this area. Although she has studied the subject at school herself, that was a long time ago and she does not feel confident enough to support pupils in Biology. She usually works in the Geography and PE departments.

● What might be a good starting point for Sinem?

● How could she use support available within the school and beyond to support her knowledge and skills?

Solution

Sinem should start by thinking about her current level of knowledge and skills in the subject and then speak to other support staff who work within the Biology department. This will help her to get an idea of what is expected rather than imagining ideas which may not be correct! She should also ask whether she can sit in on a couple of lessons as an extra support assistant so that she can gain further insight into how the subject is supported. The department as a whole may be able to offer further support as may local authority support staff training courses.

Chapter 3

🡕 **brilliant** case study

Delainey, Billy and Marisa are in the same Year 2 group for Maths. You have been asked to work with them on an activity to check their knowledge and understanding of place value. Delainey learns by looking and following instructions; Billy enjoys trying things out and having a go; Marisa listens carefully and likes to discuss what she is doing as she works.

● How do you think you might better help them by thinking about different learning styles?

● Can you think of an example of how you might take them through the activity?

Solution

In this situation you will need to be aware that as you are working with a small group you will need to clarify the concept in different ways. Place value is a concept which can take some time for pupils to understand clearly so plenty of hands-on counting and discussion using materials such as multilink or straws to make groups of 10 will make it more accessible to these pupils. You may also work with resources which are specific to place value such as place value cards, ICT programmes and so on but for all of these and with the needs of these pupils a range of different approaches will be best with plenty of opportunity for talk. As always when you are carrying out these kinds of activities you will need to discuss your approach with the teacher first.

⟋ brilliant case study

Ellie is supporting in Year 1 and has recently started working in a new school. She is an experienced assistant and has always kept stickers in her pocket to hand out to pupils. During a Maths lesson she notices that one girl is trying particularly hard and gives her a sticker. Later on the class teacher tells Ellie that stickers are never used in that particular school and that verbal praise is seen as far more powerful. Ellie is very surprised.

- What do you think about Ellie's reaction?
- Is anyone in the wrong here?
- What else could Ellie do the next time she sees the girl trying hard?

Solution

Ellie's reaction is understandable but it is important in this situation that someone in the school should take her through both the behaviour policy and also the rewards which the school uses for promoting effort. This should have been explained to her when she started in her role so it is not Ellie's fault – schools need to have clear guidelines for staff concerning the kinds of rewards which are available. The next time Ellie sees the girl trying hard she should reward her with praise, tell the teacher and follow school policy.

Chapter 4

⟋ brilliant case study

Year 2 have been in the class for almost half a term and the class teacher and teaching assistant have devised an agreed set of rules with the children which are displayed on the wall. Ralf has recently started to be ▷

spiteful to another child in the class and has said that he does not want to play with him or be his friend. The class teacher says to him, 'Ralf, we agreed as a class that we will always be kind to others.'

● Do you think that Ralf will be more likely to listen to the teacher since he helped devise the rules?

● What else could staff do to try to ensure that this kind of behaviour occurs less frequently?

Solution

Ralf should be more likely to listen to the teacher as he helped to agree the set of rules which are on display. It may be necessary to remind him of this whilst talking about how his behaviour will have made his friend feel.

Staff in the classroom should reinforce the class rules by drawing the attention of the children to them regularly and by praising the behaviour of those who are observing them, for example 'Well done, Amal, for lining up quietly'. It will also be helpful to have a whole school policy for behaviour management so that all staff know the kinds of rewards to use alongside verbal praise.

Chapter 5

brilliant case study

Andre is working in Year 1 as a general teaching assistant. A child in the class, Phoebe, has shown some causes for concern due to her speech and language, which is also impacting significantly on her ability to learn. After some discussion with the SENCO and Pheobe's parents, they have decided to give her an IEP with specific language targets. Andre has been working with Phoebe three times a week for two terms on her targets but Phoebe has made little progress. After speaking to Phoebe's parents, the SENCO and class teacher decide that they will refer Phoebe to a speech and language therapist for further assessment.

● Would Phoebe now be on School Action or School Action Plus?

Solution

Once Phoebe has been referred to the speech and language therapist or to any other professional from outside the school she will automatically go on to School Action Plus, particularly as she has made little progress after two terms on her IEP.

brilliant case study

You are working as an individual support assistant for Bhumika, who is in Year 5. She is autistic and consequently also has problems with speech and language. The autism advisory teacher comes into school once a term to observe Bhumika and to speak to you, and then separately to Bhumika's parents and the SENCO. He writes a report which gives suggested targets for Bhumika's IEP which he goes through with you and always tells you that you will have a copy. However, in the eighteen months you have been at the school you have never received a copy. You have asked the SENCO several times and although she always says that she will pass it on to you this has not happened. You can only assume that this is because she is always so busy.

● Why is it important that you should get to see the report?
● What would you do in this situation?

Solution

It is very important that you should see the report and other information concerning Bhumika's progress as you are working as her individual support assistant. You should have access to this to enable you to support her effectively. If the SENCO does not pass on the information, ask whether you can make an appointment with her to discuss Bhumika's progress formally and make a point of outlining your concerns, if necessary with another member of staff present.

Chapter 6

↗ brilliant case study

Sobiga is a new pupil in your class who does not speak any English. Although she has made friends and is involved in class activities, you have noticed that at breaktimes and lunchtimes she is often on her own.

● What kind of support does Sobiga need and why?

● List some strategies that you could use to help her to develop her self-esteem and language skills.

Solution

Sobiga needs to have some support in developing her friendships and confidence in using social language outside the classroom. It may help her on the playground or at breaks if you can encourage her to join in with playground games using equipment and facilities which are available. She could also be given a 'buddy' to look after her at these times of day. Depending on her age this may not be appropriate so if Sobiga is an older pupil you could also talk to her about going to any extra-curricular activities which are on offer at the school. The school may also offer additional support and you may be able to speak to your SENCO or English as a second language advisory teacher about the kinds of strategies which are appropriate for her.

Chapter 7

🡕 brilliant case study

Richard is working in a secondary school as an assistant in the Music department. Although the current Year 7 have not been in school for long, he has noticed that one pupil in particular, Ahsan, seems to be showing a strong talent in both piano and cello. Ahsan does not have lessons at the school but has joined the lower school orchestra and is very keen on using the piano in the music room to practice for one of his grades the following week.

- What would you do if you were Richard?
- How could you ensure that Ahsan's talent is encouraged in school?

Solution

If the Music teachers have not noticed already, Richard should draw Ahsan to their attention as a pupil who is potentially talented and encourage the development of his ability as much as possible. Although he does not have piano lessons in the school he should be encouraged to play in his free time if he can and use his talent to support the school in other ways such as in assemblies and musical concerts.

🡕 brilliant case study

Nadia is in Year 2 and is a very quiet pupil. Although you have known her for some time, you have noticed that she is becoming more confident and has started to be very quick at responding to the teacher in a range of situations. You start to observe her more carefully and within one week you are able to give several examples of situations in which she has shown a higher level of understanding than her peers.

▶

- Should you automatically assume that Nadia is a Gifted and Talented pupil?
- What should you do next?

Solution

You should not automatically assume that Nadia is a Gifted and Talented pupil although she has shown that she is working at a higher level than some of the others. It would be best to seek advice from the school's Gifted and Talented co-ordinator who will be able to carry out more assessments on Nadia and work from there.

Chapter 8

⟋ brilliant case study

Jean-Paul works in a small village primary school where the pupils usually transfer to a number of much larger secondary schools in the area. He spends his time as a teaching assistant in a mixed Year 5/6 class and is presently working with the teacher to manage the leavers' production and to ensure that the transition process goes smoothly.

- Why is it particularly important in Jean-Paul's school to manage transition actively and to reassure pupils about any concerns which they may have?
- How might Jean-Paul be involved in the process?

Solution

It is important for all schools to manage the transition from primary to secondary school actively but for a smaller primary, especially when feeding a much larger secondary school, it will help pupils to be able to discuss what their new surroundings will be like and how teaching and learning will be different. They should also have opportunities to visit the school and discuss issues such as travelling to school, managing homework, and organisation skills. Jean-Paul may be involved in the process in a number of ways, from taking out individuals or small groups to discuss worries that they may not want to talk about in front of the class, to working with Year 7 teachers to discuss common issues.

brilliant case study

Sally works as a teaching assistant in Year 5, whose topic at present is 'What is my carbon footprint?' She has been working with the class to try to think of ways to save energy and encourage others to do the same. As part of this project they have decided to write to the local council and ask them to review recycling in the borough's schools to include more materials as at the moment they just recycle paper.

- How will this idea support community cohesion as well as enhancing what the pupils are doing as part of the curriculum?

Solution

This project will support community cohesion as it will form links with the local area and show pupils how their learning is linked to real life situations. They are also likely to be motivated by the fact that they are able to work together to make a difference. This can also be extended in other ways such as writing to local newspapers and asking other schools to support their idea.

brilliant case study

Amal has been working in a secondary school for four months and is based in Years 7 and 8. He has been trained in restorative justice techniques at ▶

his previous school and also speaks Hindu. There have been some cases of racist bullying amongst the girls in the two year groups during breaktimes and Amal suggests to the head of Year 7 that he should run some sessions.

● What should Amal do first?

● What kind of form could the sessions take?

Solution

Amal should make sure that he speaks to all sides concerned and be clear on exactly what has happened so that he can tackle the situation carefully. He should invite the two sides to come and discuss what has happened, and act as an interpreter in his language if needed. Depending on the number of pupils involved he may need to run several sessions with different pupils.

Chapter 9

⤴ brilliant case study

Gina has just started a job in a new primary school. She is regularly on playground duty and notices that staff often carry cups of tea and coffee outside, particularly in colder weather. They are also able to take hot drinks to their classrooms. Gina is very alert to this as in her previous school there was an accident in which a pupil suffered serious burns after running into an adult who was carrying a hot drink. As she is new she does not wish to appear to be a killjoy; however, she is anxious that the same thing does not happen again.

● Should Gina say anything?

● Can you think of a way in which this could be resolved without upsetting other staff?

Solution

Gina should say something in confidence, either to the headteacher or the school's health and safety officer. It may be that the school had not considered the dangers of allowing staff to do this. If the school then forbids carrying hot drinks she will not be seen as responsible. One suggestion is sharing breaktimes so that two teachers cover – for example, in a 20-minute break there are two ten-minute shifts to allow each person to have a drink and comfort break. Alternatively, schools might decide to allow staff to carry hot drinks if they are in high-sided boxes so that any spills do not present a hazard to others.

brilliant case study

Janine is working as a cover supervisor in Key Stage 3. She does not work with all the pupils as she tends to cover Maths and Music lessons, but this involves working with the same pupils each week. She has been approached by a pupil in Year 9 who has said that she is worried about her friend in her class whose father is an alcoholic – she says that her friend has confided in her that he is sometimes violent with both her and her mother.

- What should Janine do first?
- What should she say to the pupil?

Solution

It is important that Janine should ask the pupil to talk to her about what has happened whilst not pressing her or asking her leading questions. She should also emphasise that she will need to tell someone else in order to keep the pupil safe. She should write down everything that the pupil tells her, as soon after as possible, so that she is able to remember any details. She should then speak to the school's child protection or safeguarding officer as soon as possible.

Chapter 10

brilliant case study

Saskia is an experienced support assistant and in addition has just started to run a small craft club for Key Stage 2 after school. She has the use of a classroom and has a group of 12 children for the activities. Saskia has taken a register of pupils at the beginning so knows who is present but, following the club, one of the Year 6 children tells her that she is allowed to walk home on her own. Ten minutes later her mother comes to collect her and although she is late tells Saskia that she did not give her permission to walk home and will be speaking to the headteacher straight away.

- How should Saskia have responded to the girl's request?
- What should she do now to support the parent?

Solution

If the girl did not have written permission with her, Saskia should have asked the pupil to wait until she was able to check with the child's teacher or the school office and explain why. It is important that she supports the parent by taking her to the headteacher and then trying to trace the girl in whatever way is decided by the group.

brilliant case study

James runs the local scout group and the venue he has been using has just told him that they will be unable to carry on using it due to building work over the next few months. As he also works at the local secondary school as a member of support staff, he has had the idea of booking the school hall and also offering Duke of Edinburgh award training to pupils from the surrounding area as an extra activity.

● Would James be able to do this?

● Where might he go for support in order to see his idea through?

Solution

James may be able to do this if it is agreed by the school. He should then approach surrounding schools to gauge the level of interest – it may be that he has too many pupils to offer to a wider number. He could also talk to others in local schools who run clubs and extended school activities for additional support and can contact them through his local authority.

Chapter 11

⟳ brilliant case study

Jackie is working as an individual support assistant for a blind pupil in a secondary school. She has been there for two years and, although she is very experienced and well trained for her work with the pupil, she does not have any qualifications. She has been investigating some of her options – she would like to be better qualified as there is a possibility that her pupil may be moving schools. However, she does not have much contact with her line manager as she is not full time, and there are no points of contact during the week.

● What should Jackie do first?

● Is there anything else she could do if the school could not support her request?

Solution

Jackie should first of all speak to her line manager to find out whether the school will support her and if there is any training available. If for some reason they are unable to (for example, if there is nothing available which will fit with her timetable or they are unable to let her out of school in lesson times) she may need to find out about evening classes through her local college or through the local authority.

Appendix 2: Teacher/TA feedback sheet

Teacher/TA Feedback Sheet

To be filled in by teacher: Class:
Teacher's name:
TA's name:

Brief description of activity

How session is linked to medium-term plans

TA's role

Important vocabulary

Key learning points

For use during group work:

Children	D	H	Feedback/Assessment

D = Can do task
H = Help required to complete task

Source: Burnham, L. (2007) *S/NVQ Level 3 The Teaching Assistant's Handbook: Primary Schools*

Glossary

AfL	Assessment for Learning
ASD	Autistic Spectrum Disorder
BSP	Behaviour Support Plan
COP	Code of Practice
CPD	Continuing Professional Development
DCSF	Department for Children, Schools and Families
DFE	Department for Education
DfES	Department for Education and Skills (old name for the DCSF)
EP	Educational psychologist
EYFS	Early Years Foundation Stage
G & T	Gifted and Talented
HLTA	Higher Level Teaching Assistant
IEP	Individual Education Plan
INSET	In Service Education and Training
ISA	Individual support assistant
LA	Local authority

LSA	Learning support assistant
NAPTA	National Association of Professional Teaching Assistants
NQT	Newly qualified teacher
NVQ	National Vocational Qualification
OT	Occupational therapist
PPA	Planning, preparation and assessment
PSP	Personal Support Plan
SALT/SLT	Speech and language therapist
SDP	School development plan
SEN	Special educational needs
SENCO	Special Educational Needs Co-Ordinator
SMT/SLT	Senior Management Team/Senior Leadership Team
SSSNB	School Support Staff Negotiating Body
SWiS	Support Work in Schools qualification
TDA	Training and Development Agency for Schools

Index